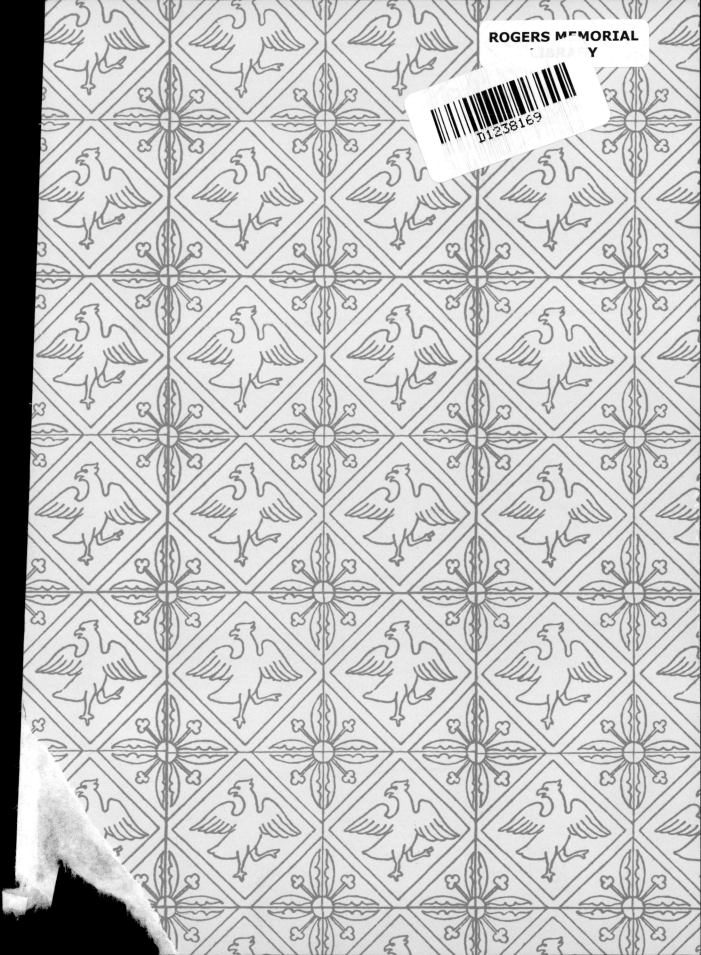

# BISOUS &
# BRIOCHE

# BISOUS & BRIOCHE

*Classic French Recipes and Family*
*Favorites from a Life in France*

LAURA BRADBURY
and
REBECCA WELLMAN

Photography by REBECCA WELLMAN

TOUCHWOOD

*For Renate.*
*My sister in all the most important ways.*
—RW

*This is for my wonderful readers and for all the people*
*in France who have fed me incredible meals.*
—LB

*bisou* [bizu] *(familier)*
*nom masculin*
**kiss**

*donne-moi ou fais-moi un bisou*
**give me a kiss**

—*LAROUSSE DICTIONNAIRE*

# CONTENTS

# INTRODUCTION

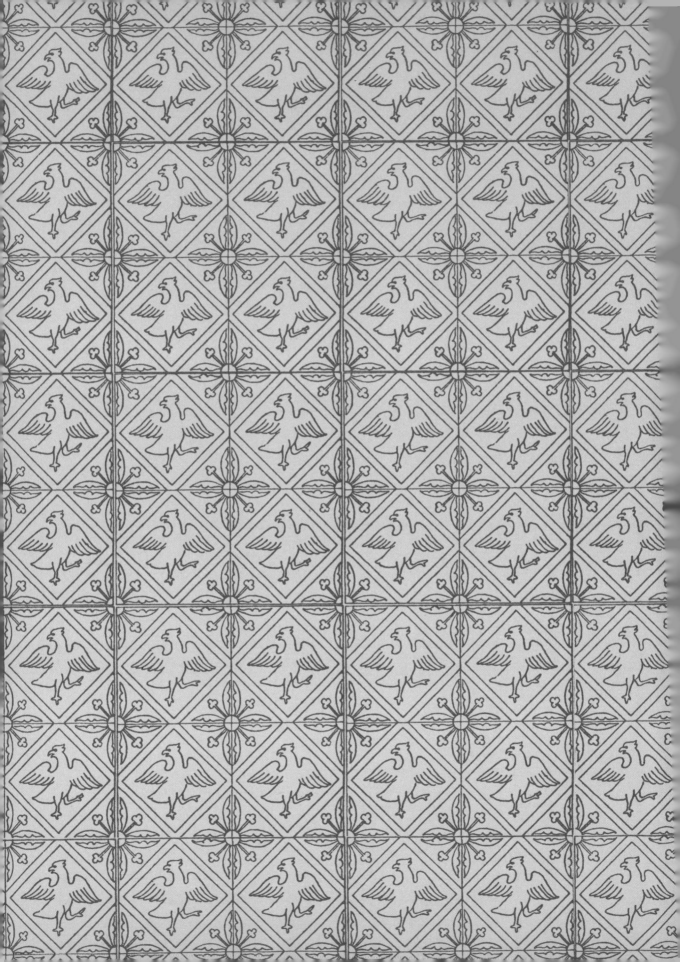

# INTRODUCTION

—LAURA BRADBURY

I NEVER THOUGHT I WOULD WRITE A COOKBOOK. In fact, my family dissolves into hysterics every time I mention this fact. Then again, I never thought I would speak fluent French, marry a Frenchman, own vacation rentals in the vineyards of Burgundy, or become a full-time writer.

I never cease to be amazed by life and those instants that turn your entire world on its axis in a matter of seconds. Such a moment happened for me when my local Rotary Club decided on the spur of the moment to send me to France instead of Belgium for my exchange year after high school.

That single decision defined the entire course of my existence. Over the course of a year in Burgundy I learned French, became enamored with the local food and wine, and most importantly, fell in love with my future husband, a Frenchman named, appropriately, Franck.

For those of you who haven't yet discovered my memoirs, the short version is that *oui*, Franck and I soon realized in classic romance fashion we wanted to be together forever. Not everyone, however, was as enthused about this idea as we were. My parents were horrified I was moving in with an unknown Frenchman several years older than me, and Franck's parents didn't understand why he couldn't just settle down with a nice village lass instead of leaving them to be with a girl who came from a vast, untamed country where wild beasts roamed.

Neverthless, we fought to be together, despite everyone's belief that we could never make it work. Besides family opposition, we had to run the gauntlet of mafia landlords, real estate crooks, seemingly impossible immigration hurdles, and perilous jobs—which involved getting lost on the Pacific Ocean in the fog—as well as near-death experiences and disappearing priests, among countless other obstacles, in order to stay together.

Our romance spanned Burgundy, Montreal, Victoria, Alaska, Paris, Nepal, and Oxford. Luckily, we were both in it for the long run and went on to restore four old houses (plus a 13th-century wine cellar under the streets of Beaune) in the Burgundian vineyards and convert them to vacation rentals. After we finished that, I began to record our story in my Grape Series memoirs. In between, we managed to have three daughters and adopt a rescue dog. My family came to be because the Rotary decided on a whim to send me to France, and it is this very same family who laugh at the notion I'm co-authoring a cookbook.

It's not that I'm terrible in the kitchen, although I do have some cooking disasters (some unfortunately involving fire extinguishers) to my name that form part of our family lore. I would classify myself as an intimidated cook, especially among the legendary chefs in Franck's family who can all whip up a gourmet French meal at a moment's notice. My cooking skills are not rated particularly high by Franck and our family and friends in France, so the news that I was co-authoring a cookbook struck them as hilarious. I have to admit that it even feels a bit absurd to me. I am a storyteller first and foremost. I never set out to be a cookbook writer. I do, however, believe that cooking is yet another (very delicious) form of storytelling.

I am perfectly positioned to relate to other intimidated cooks—and to share some of my secrets for feeling more confident in the kitchen. Over time, I slowly collected a quiverful of French recipes that I could consistently knock out of the park and that always earned accolades from even the staunchest of my French critics (and the French are not shy about offering criticism). These recipes came from friends and family, and sometimes even a ripped-out magazine article I adapted for my purposes. I committed most of these recipes to memory so that I had a respectable repertoire at my fingertips. This is my main tip for anyone who feels anxious about cooking: build a recipe bank, no matter how small, of dishes that you can master. This was the single most helpful thing that allowed me, as an intimidated cook, to become more confident. You'll find my recipe bank (plus a few extras) within the pages of this book.

Unlike cooking, I've always been a natural-born genius at eating. As my dear French friend Marie declared at a recent dinner together, "Maybe Laura isn't the best at cooking, but she is certainly the best at *eating*!"

Indeed, I am known among our friends and family in France as a *gourmande*, meaning a person who has a marked enthusiasm and appreciation for good food. *Bien sûr*, as I mentioned earlier, I am principally a storyteller, but because I am a *gourmande* storyteller, my memoirs are packed full of descriptions of the meals I have been privileged to enjoy in my many years in France. My readers tell me these descriptions make their mouths water and inspire them to cook up a storm.

As my Grape Series attracted more and more readers, the chorus of demands for a cookbook grew louder. My readers wanted to recreate the French dishes I wrote so lovingly about in my memoirs. There was only one problem: with all the will in the world, I was neither a confident cook nor a food photographer. . . . I had no idea where to begin such a project.

Luckily, Rebecca came to the rescue. I had known her for several years through the foodie community of Victoria, British Columbia, Canada, which is where I live when I'm not in Burgundy, and greatly admired her photography in local publications. She also published a wonderful brunch cookbook titled *First, We Brunch* a few years ago through TouchWood Editions. It began to dawn on me that I had perhaps found the perfect person to collaborate with.

Rebecca and I shared a vision of a cookbook based on my memoirs that was both visually stunning and accessible—a cookbook that felt friendly and fun for the home cook, even those with a few kitchen disasters to their name like *moi*. French recipes are perceived to be complicated and time-consuming. Some of them are, but the arsenal of dishes inside this book is proof that you can master French cooking without shedding a year's worth of tears or spending hours in the kitchen (although there are a few exceptions, such as cannelés, but they're so delicious they're worth the extra work).

We set out to create a cookbook that feels just as welcoming as a family meal in Burgundy. Rebecca and I started with my own collection of French recipes as the skeleton of *Bisous & Brioche*, then we branched out into recipes I had tasted in France and dreamed of adding to my kitchen repertoire. She adapted and perfected them, and even created many wonderful new ones that I have already incorporated into my life. She developed, cooked, styled, and photographed all the recipes in this book.

We struggled for months to find a title for our cookbook that encapsulated the warmth of a home-cooked French meal enjoyed with loved ones. The word *bisous* may not be well known in North America, but in France it covered all our bases and more. *Bisous* are the welcome and farewell kisses that are part of life all over France, but the word is also what you would call out to a friend or use to sign off a letter or phone call to a loved one to express your affection and appreciation for having that person in your life. *Bisous* conveys warmth, welcome, and love.

As for the *brioche* part, Rebecca took my idea of a *brioche* recipe for the cookbook and ran with it, creating the most stunning and delicious honey-glazed brioche. That brioche is one of our star recipes and illustrates the magical synergy of the collaboration between the two of us. Besides, the writer in me loves the alliteration.

You'll notice most of the recipe titles in this cookbook are in English rather than their original French. This is because this is a book about good food, not about learning all the French terms for that food. You don't need to speak French to immerse yourself in France's culinary culture. Our goal with *Bisous & Brioche* is always to reduce the intimidation factor. There is plenty of inspiration within these pages to provide you with the warm embrace of countless pleasurable hours around a table with *gourmands* you would give a *bisou* to. After all, that's what life is for, *n'est-ce pas?*

As you browse through the recipes in this book, you'll find that many of them call for staple items, such as herbes de Provence or a special kind of French pastry, which are recipes in their own right. These form the backbone of French cooking and are the sort of things that every French cook either has in their pantry or knows how to whip up easily. We've grouped all these staples—and more!—in this chapter so they're easy to refer back to, make in advance, and store for frequent use. If you work through these recipes, building up a collection of staples, you will have your very own French pantry. *À vos tabliers, prêts, partez!*

# INSIDE THE
# FRENCH PANTRY

# A PRIMER ON INGREDIENTS

Before you launch yourself into the recipes, here's a tried and tested list of basic ingredients to keep in your fridge or pantry so that you're ready for (almost) anything in the kitchen.

One of the things I've learned in my decades of cooking is that, maybe with the exception of baking, a recipe is but a guideline. This is my greatest challenge when writing recipes—I don't want to be too bossy. Dishes can be modified, depending on what you are in the mood for, what is in the pantry, and who is coming for dinner, and I fully encourage you to make the recipes in this book your own. In saying that, I do have some preferences for certain ingredients for the recipes in this book. And when it comes to oil, vinegar, Dijon mustard (see page 33), and Puy lentils, buy the best possible quality you can afford.—RW

---

**ALLIUMS** While onions, leeks, and shallots all have their own distinct flavors, ranging from very strong to quite mild, they can replace one another in a pinch.

**BUTTER** Use unsalted unless otherwise specified.

**CHOCOLATE** There is no comparison to high-quality chocolate. Spend the extra money. You won't be sorry.

**CITRUS** Freshly squeezed citrus juices, such as lemon, are always recommended, but if you are in a pinch and you have a bottle of quality pure lemon juice on hand, feel free to use it. I would not recommend using the plastic lemon-shaped squeeze bottles, as their contents typically lack the flavor of fresh juice.

**DAIRY** When combining dairy and acid (such as lemon juice or vinegar) in a recipe, full-fat dairy is required to keep the dish from curdling. In recipes where this isn't a factor, feel free to use whatever milk or yogurt you have in the fridge.

**DIJON MUSTARD** When Dijon is called for in a recipe, I mean smooth. Grainy will be specified if that is the better option, but if smooth is all you have, go for it!

**EGGS** The recipes in this book have been written with large eggs in mind.

**HERBS** Fresh herbs are definitely superior to their dried counterparts, and where it seems somewhat essential to the success of the dish, I've specified fresh in the ingredients list. I do understand, however, that where you live and what time of

year it is will affect your access to fresh herbs, so use your discretion here. As a general rule, if you are replacing fresh herbs with dried in your recipe, use about one third of the amount, as dried herbs have a much more concentrated flavor than fresh. For example, to replace 1 tablespoon of fresh thyme, use 1 teaspoon of dried.

MAPLE SYRUP Here is where I will get bossy. The highest, purest grade is always recommended, and Aunt Jemima is no substitute.

OLIVE OIL This is such a personal preference, as olive oils can vary greatly in spiciness and fruitiness. For dressings, I prefer a mild-tasting olive oil, allowing the other ingredients to shine through. Go with your favorite on this one.

PARSLEY Curly or flat-leaf can be used interchangeably, depending on your taste preferences. Flat-leaf parsley is typically known to be slightly stronger in flavor, but that depends greatly on the plant itself. Go with what is most easily available and what looks best on the plate.

PEPPER I use freshly ground black pepper (sometimes with some white and pink peppercorns thrown into the mix). Unless salt or pepper is an actual measured ingredient in a recipe, I have left them off the ingredients list but included them in the method, so you can season to taste with no exact rules.

SALT My two favorite pantry salts are sea salt and kosher salt. Sea salt, or fleur de sel, is great for finishing dishes. Kosher salt is best for salting water before boiling or salting meat before browning, as it's typically less expensive and its large flakes hold onto moisture better, making for a more tender piece of meat. The local grocery store in Beaune has a heady selection of fleur de sel from different salt-producing areas of France—the Camargue, Brittany, and Normandy, for example—but no matter where it's from, fleur de sel is harvested from the young crystals that form on top of salt evaporation ponds. It is the most delicate-tasting salt available and a pinch of it elevates every recipe, from a sweet pastry to a coq au vin.

VEGETABLE OIL For cooking, a high-smoke-point oil is recommended, such as grapeseed, avocado, or canola.

# SEASONINGS

I distinctly remember one of my first meals in France with my first host family in Burgundy. It was a fresh zucchini soup, followed by roasted leg of lamb with herbes de Provence. I marveled at how everything just tasted so good. Even foods I thought I didn't particularly like tasted delicious in France. My host brother shrugged and said, "Of course food needs to taste good. Otherwise, why eat?"

This was a revelation for me. I had been brought up believing that foods that were good for me generally tasted bland or just outright bad (think boiled broccoli or lamb chops with mint jelly). We ate those things because they were good for us, not for pleasure. In France, cooking was about making all food taste delicious. Seasonings such as the ones below played a huge part.

---

## Bouquet Garni
### MAKES ONE

To make a bouquet garni, gather a few stalks of any of the fresh herbs that your recipe requires. This could be a combination of any of the herbs listed here.

Tie the stalks together with kitchen twine or, if you are using smaller herbs and spices such as peppercorns, fold the herbs and spices up into a little package, wrap them in muslin or cheese cloth, and tie them in a little bundle or secure with kitchen twine. This whole package gets plopped into your soup, stew, or sauce and infuses its distinct French flavors into your dish. Remove it once the dish is done and *voilà*: your dish has a delicious herbaceous flavor without any little leaves floating in it.

parsley

bay leaves

thyme

rosemary

peppercorns

tarragon

basil

chervil

savory

---

## Quatre Épices
### MAKES ABOUT 2 TBSP

Make a batch of this by combining the ingredients and storing in a sealed container for up to a year. This is the French version of allspice and it gives a deep, earthy flavor to terrines, stews, and dishes like duck confit.

1 Tbsp ground white pepper

1½ tsp ground ginger

1½ tsp ground cloves

1½ tsp ground nutmeg

# Herbes de Provence

**MAKES ABOUT ½ CUP**

Treat this list of ingredients as a guideline. Mix and match, increasing or decreasing quantities according to taste. Combine and store in a cool, dry place. Rubbed into a chicken before roasting, added to meatballs before cooking, or sprinkled on top of potatoes cooked any which way, there is no other ingredient (okay, except perhaps bouquet garni) to make everything taste like France. I've never met a French cook, from the humblest to the Michelin-starred, who doesn't have herbes de Provence in their kitchen.

You can even try this with fresh herbs, although they'll need to be used right away. If you replace fresh herbs for the dried in a recipe, be sure to use three times the amount, as the herbs are more concentrated once dried.

2 Tbsp dried thyme

2 Tbsp dried savory

1 Tbsp dried oregano or marjoram

1 Tbsp dried rosemary

2 Tbsp dried parsley

1 Tbsp dried lavender

*A bouquet garni made from fresh herbs is best used immediately. However, you can also stir together dried herbs in the measurements you desire and keep them in a jar. Experiment with this option and make it your own! It's not a bad mixture to have in the pantry, and it will keep for up to a year in a cool, dry spot away from light. Rule of thumb: if your herbs or spices have reached their first birthday, it's best to replace them.*—RW

# DRESSINGS AND VINAIGRETTES

When I go into a grocery store and see a wall of premade dressings, all I can think is why? Homemade vinaigrette was the first thing I learned to make in France. I remember my first host mother—the incredibly chic Mme Beaupré—teaching me her recipe with three ingredients and only a fork and a small glass bowl for equipment. Her kitchen in Nuits-Saint-Georges was still warm from the late summer sun, and we were making a large green salad to have for lunch in the garden. I haven't had a bottle of store-bought dressing in my kitchen since then.

## Mme Beaupré's Homemade Vinaigrette
**MAKES 1½ CUPS**

In a Mason jar, measuring cup, or glass bowl, whisk together the Dijon and vinegar.

Very, very slowly, drizzle in the oil while whisking vigorously until well blended.

Mix in the shallot and tarragon (if using), and season to taste with sea salt and pepper. The dressing will keep in the fridge for 4–5 days.

¼ cup grainy or smooth Dijon mustard

2 Tbsp champagne or white wine vinegar

1 cup mild-tasting olive oil or grapeseed oil

1 shallot, finely minced

1 Tbsp finely minced tarragon (optional)

## Blue Cheese Dressing
**MAKES 2 CUPS**

Place the cheese, chives, onion powder, sour cream, buttermilk, lemon juice, and Worcestershire sauce in a food processor or blender. Blend until the mixture is creamy and combined. Taste and season with sea salt and pepper. This dressing is best if you allow it to sit, covered, in the fridge for a couple of hours so the flavors meld. The dressing will keep in the fridge for 4–5 days.

5 oz blue cheese, crumbled (Gorgonzola or Stilton are good options)

2 Tbsp minced chives

1 tsp onion powder

½ cup sour cream

½ cup buttermilk

2 Tbsp lemon juice

Dash of Worcestershire sauce

# Raspberry Vinaigrette

**MAKES 1½ CUPS**

Place the raspberries, basil, and vinegar in a food processor or blender. Pulse until the berries and basil are well chopped. In a very slow and steady stream, add the oil while the machine is running, until the mixture is emulsified and creamy. Season generously with sea salt and pepper. The dressing will keep in the fridge for 4–5 days.

¾ cup fresh or frozen (thawed) raspberries

2 Tbsp chopped basil leaves

¼ cup apple cider vinegar

1 tsp balsamic vinegar

½ cup mild-tasting olive oil or grapeseed oil

---

# Maple-Dijon Vinaigrette

**MAKES 1½ CUPS**

In a Mason jar or measuring cup, whisk together the garlic, vinegar, Dijon, and maple syrup. Very, very slowly, drizzle in the oil while whisking vigorously until well blended. Season to taste with sea salt and pepper. The dressing will keep in the fridge for 4–5 days.

1 large garlic clove, finely minced

6 Tbsp champagne or white wine vinegar

2 Tbsp Dijon mustard

1 Tbsp + 2 tsp grade A maple syrup

1 cup mild-tasting olive oil or grapeseed oil

---

# Creamy Herb Dressing

**MAKES 1½ CUPS**

Place the scallions, garlic, dill, basil, and parsley in a food processor or blender. Pulse until the garlic and scallions are minced. Add the buttermilk, yogurt, oil, and lemon juice, season with sea salt and pepper, and blend to combine. The mixture should be smooth. This is best if you allow it to sit, covered, in the fridge for a couple of hours so the flavors meld. The dressing will keep in the fridge for 3–4 days.

3 scallions, roughly chopped

1 small garlic clove, roughly chopped

1 Tbsp chopped dill

1 Tbsp chopped basil

1 Tbsp chopped parsley

¾ cup buttermilk

½ cup Greek yogurt

¼ cup mild-tasting olive oil or grapeseed oil

1 Tbsp lemon juice

# Balsamic Vinaigrette

**MAKES 1½ CUPS**

In a Mason jar or measuring cup, whisk together the shallot, garlic, balsamic, honey, and Dijon.

Very, very slowly, drizzle in the oil while whisking vigorously until well blended.

Stir in the thyme and season with sea salt and pepper. The dressing will keep in the fridge for 4–5 days.

1 shallot, minced

1 garlic clove, minced

½ cup balsamic vinegar

4 tsp honey

2 tsp Dijon mustard

1 cup mild-tasting olive oil or grapeseed oil

2 tsp minced thyme leaves

# STOCKS AND BROTHS

Stock need not be intimidating or difficult. Whenever I roast a whole organic chicken, I throw the carcass into the freezer along with any of the juices that are left over once the meat has been removed from the bones. When I am need of some stock, I simply set the frozen carcass and juices in a large stockpot on the stove and let it simmer through the day. This applies to organic beef bones, too! The recipes below will make a varying amount, upward of 10 cups or so, depending on how much water gets added in the end. I like to keep stocks and broths fairly simple to start, modifying with extra herbs and spices, citrus, or tomato paste as I use it with the dish I am making or simply to suit my current mood. All stocks will keep in the freezer for up to 3 months. —RW

## Beef Stock

### MAKES 2–3 LITRES

Heat the oven to 450°F. Line a rimmed sheet pan with parchment paper.

Lay the bones out on the prepared pan and slather with the tomato paste. Season generously with kosher salt and pepper. Roast in the oven until the bones are dark and caramelized, 25–35 minutes.

Place the bones in a large stockpot and add the carrots, celery, onions, garlic, thyme, parsley stems, bay leaves, and peppercorns. Pour about 12 cups of water over top and bring to a gentle boil. Immediately turn down the heat to a simmer and skim off any scum from the surface. Be sure not to let the mixture boil (just simmer) and continue to skim when necessary. Simmer, uncovered, for 5–6 hours, stirring occasionally and adding another cup or two of water if it's simmered away to below the level of the bones and vegetables. Season to taste with sea salt (I would start with 2 tsp, then add more if necessary).

Remove from the heat and let cool almost completely. Strain through a sieve into various sizes of sterilized Mason jars and discard the solids.

5 lb veal or beef marrow bones

3 Tbsp tomato paste

4 carrots, roughly chopped

4 celery stalks, roughly chopped

2 onions, halved

6–8 cloves of garlic, peeled

4 sprigs thyme

½ bunch flat-leaf parsley stems (see note)

4 bay leaves

½ tsp black peppercorns

*Parsley stems have a more intense flavor than their leafy counterparts. In a broth or stock, their hardier texture can handle the long cooking time without tasting overcooked. Throwing them into a big pot of stock is a great way to use up those typically tossed-out bits! —RW*

# Chicken Stock

**MAKES 2–3 LITRES**

Place the chicken carcasses in a large stockpot, and add the onions, carrots, celery, bay leaves, and peppercorns. Pour about 12 cups of water over top, give it a stir, and bring to a gentle boil over high heat. Immediately turn down the heat to a simmer and skim off any scum from the surface. Be sure not to let the mixture boil (just simmer) and continue to skim as necessary.

Simmer, uncovered, for 4–5 hours, stirring occasionally and adding another cup or two of water if it's simmered away to below the level of the bones and vegetables. The bones should be cleanish when it's ready. Season to taste with sea salt (I would start with 2 tsp, then add more if necessary).

Remove from the heat and let cool almost completely. Strain through a sieve into various sizes of sterilized Mason jars and discard the solids. Feel free to add more herbs (closer to the end of simmering), some citrus, grated ginger, or whole smashed garlic cloves if you like.

1–2 roasted chicken carcasses

1 large onion, peeled and quartered

2 carrots, roughly chopped

2 celery stalks, including leaves, roughly chopped

3 bay leaves

½ tsp black peppercorns

---

# Vegetable Broth

**MAKES 2–3 LITRES**

Heat the oven to 450°F. Line two large rimmed sheet pans with parchment paper.

Toss the onions, garlic, celery, carrots, fennel, and leeks with the oil, season generously with sea salt and pepper, and arrange on the two prepared sheet pans. Roast until lightly browned, about 20 minutes, tossing at the 10-minute point.

Scoop the vegetables into a large stockpot and cover with about 12 cups of water. Bring to a soft boil over high heat, then add the parsley stems, ginger, bay leaves, and peppercorns. Simmer, uncovered, for about 2 hours, stirring occasionally and adding another cup or two of water if it's simmered away to below the level of the vegetables. Season to taste with sea salt.

Remove from the heat and let cool almost completely. Strain through a sieve into various sizes of sterilized Mason jars, pressing on the vegetables with the back of a spoon to extract all their juices. Discard the solids.

1 large onion, peeled and chopped into 1-inch pieces (don't bother peeling if you don't mind a darker broth)

1 head garlic, halved (don't bother peeling)

5 stalks celery, chopped into 1-inch pieces

3 carrots, chopped into 1-inch pieces

1 small fennel bulb, chopped into 1-inch pieces

1 large leek, rinsed and white and light-green parts roughly chopped

1 Tbsp olive oil

1 small bunch parsley stems

1-inch piece of fresh ginger, peeled and roughly chopped

2 bay leaves

½ tsp black peppercorns

# SAUCES

Sauces are often the first thing people think of when you mention French cooking—and sometimes not in a good way. There is frequently an assumption that sauces make for a heavy, overly rich cusine. *C'est faux!* In this section you'll discover that what sauces add is flavor—flavor that elevates your dish from the ho-hum to the *délicieux*. Another misconception is that sauces require a certain skill to pull off, but they're not actually that complicated and they provide a huge bang for your cooking time. Master this collection of sauces and use them to your heart's content. You will be thrilled to discover how they can catapult your dishes into the taste stratosphere.

---

## Pistou

**MAKES ABOUT 1½ CUPS**

If we were to get traditional, we would be smashing salt and garlic in a mortar and pestle, adding basil, and drizzling in the olive oil. And we still can, of course, but using a food processor is entirely acceptable as well. Pistou doesn't traditionally have Parmesan in it, but it does add a lovely nutty, salty flavor. If you'd like to stick with tradition, go ahead and leave it out. Pistou is a wonderful accompaniment to crudités or toasted baguette; drizzled on top of soup or tossed with hot pasta.—RW

Place the basil and garlic in a food processor and pulse until roughly minced.

Add the lemon juice and Parmesan (if using) and process again until the cheese is incorporated, about 10 seconds. In a very slow and steady stream, drizzle in the oil while the machine is running until it is well blended. Season generously with sea salt and pepper.

3 cups packed fresh basil leaves

1 large garlic clove, roughly chopped

1 Tbsp lemon juice

¼ cup grated Parmesan cheese (optional)

½ cup extra virgin olive oil

# Béchamel Sauce

MAKES ABOUT 4 CUPS

Oh, how I adore a well-executed béchamel sauce! It is seriously one of the most comforting and versatile things in the world.

Before I moved to France, I thought making a béchamel sauce from scratch was the stuff of Cordon Bleu chefs, but after only a few months of living there, it dawned on me that every French person I had met could whip one up *sans problème*.

One day, determined to make one of my very favorite French dishes—braised endives rolled in ham covered in béchamel sauce (page 151)—I threw my wooden spoon in the ring. No one was more shocked than me when my sauce turned out smooth, thick, and delicious, and perfectly spiced with freshly grated nutmeg.

I make béchamel all the time now as a sauce base or just to enjoy poured over some cooked veggies, sprinkled with cheese, and broiled for a few minutes. I'm not going to lie; I imagine a white chef's hat perched on my head every time I do.

¼ cup butter

¼ cup all-purpose flour

½ tsp sea salt

4 cups whole milk, divided

2 tsp freshly grated nutmeg

In a medium-sized saucepan over medium-low heat, melt the butter. Make a light roux by whisking in the flour and salt, then stirring constantly with a wooden spoon until the mixture is well combined and light golden, 3–5 minutes. It should be wet, like a thick paste, but not runny.

In a slow and steady stream, whisk in 2 cups of the milk. Continue to whisk until the mixture is smooth and the milk is hot, but not boiling. Slowly add the remainder of the milk, stirring continuously so the sauce doesn't stick to the bottom of the pan. Bring the sauce to just below the boil and simmer gently until it has thickened enough to coat the back of a spoon, 5–10 minutes.

Remove from the heat and stir in the nutmeg. The sauce can be stored in the fridge for a day or two and reheated at a low temperature. Be sure to whisk it constantly as it warms through.

---

# Lemon Aioli

MAKES ABOUT 1 CUP

**Mayonnaise can be a great replacement for aioli, yes, but once you've tried this recipe, you will see that nothing beats a fresh aioli. This one is wonderful without any taste embellishments with crudités, in sandwiches and salads, or drizzled over roasted vegetables, but you can also add fresh herbs or spices to suit your tastes.—RW**

1 large clove garlic

1 tsp sea salt

1 large egg yolk

1 cup light-tasting olive oil, or ½ cup extra virgin olive oil + ½ cup vegetable oil

1 Tbsp lemon juice

1 tsp grated lemon zest

In a food processor or high-speed blender, chop the garlic. Add the salt and egg yolk and process just to combine, about 10 seconds. With the machine running, drizzle in the oil in the thinnest stream possible. Continue until the oil has all been incorporated and the mixture has thickened to the consistency of mayonnaise. Add the lemon juice and zest and blend again for 10 seconds just to incorporate. Aioli will keep in an airtight container in the fridge for 3–4 days.

# Crème Fraîche

**MAKES ABOUT 2 CUPS**

During my five years in France, I realized that crème fraîche—a delectable French cream that we used multiple times a day (and that goes perfectly in a quiche batter or dolloped on top of a bowl of freshly picked strawberries)—is one of those precious things that, like pain au chocolat fresh out of the *boulanger*'s oven and a chilled bottle of rosé on a hot summer's day, make life worth living.

Crème fraîche lives in the huge majority of French fridges, but when I moved back to North America I couldn't find any I liked, so I devised this easy and delicious homemade version. I make up a Mason jarful of it pretty much every week and keep it in my fridge. Tempted? Of course you are, otherwise you wouldn't be reading this book.

The longer you leave the crème fraîche at room temperature the sourer it will become. I love sour, tangy tastes, so I go the full 24 hours, but if you would like it a bit milder, put it in the fridge at the 12-hour mark. Here *chez nous* we enjoy crème fraîche on our pasta, in our quiches, and in sauces, and I will be using it to make a tarte au citron to take to my sister's for dinner on Friday night. *Voilà!* From now on, not living in France is no excuse for denying yourself one of the country's most versatile and delicious ingredients.

2 cups whipping cream

2 Tbsp cultured plain yogurt or buttermilk

Stir together the cream and yogurt (or buttermilk) in a jar. Cover with a clean dishtowel and let sit at room temperature for 12–24 hours, until it reaches your desired thickness and sourness. Crème fraîche will keep in an airtight container in the fridge for up to 2 weeks.

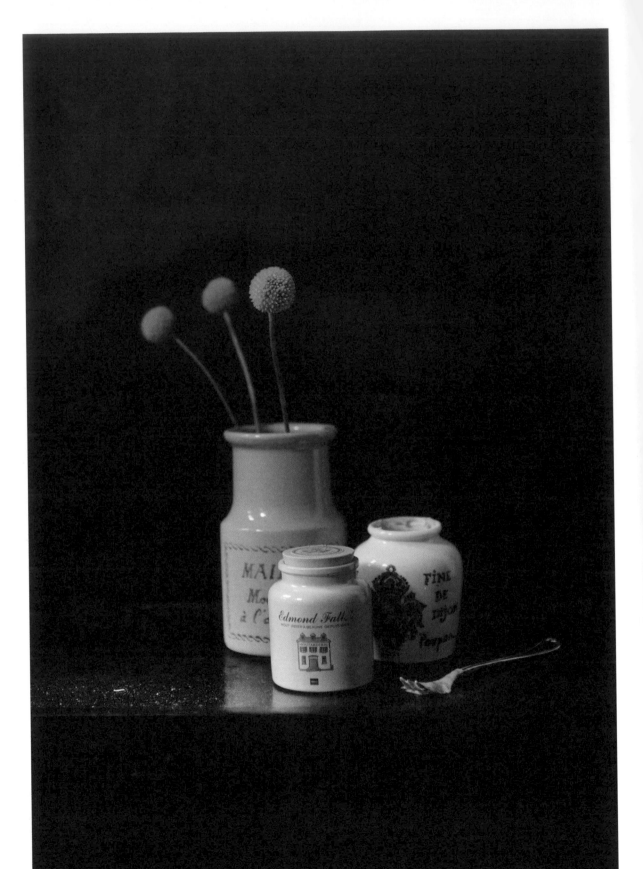

# THE MAGIC OF DIJON MUSTARD

THE FULL GLORY AND VERSATILITY OF DIJON MUSTARD didn't reveal itself to me until I arrived in Burgundy, but when it did it was like a religious conversion. The first time I saw it used was at my first host family's dinner table. I noticed they would all take a little spoonful of Dijon from the ceramic pot that always occupied a central position on the table whenever they ate meat of any kind.

I was tentative the first time they suggested I try it, but from that first forkful of turkey breast dabbed with a bit of Dijon mustard, I was a convert. Dijon is a delicate mix of spices and heat that provides the perfect foil to all kinds of food—not just meat. No Burgundian table is complete without a pot or jar of Dijon at its center. Besides, my husband was born in Dijon, so there's that too.

Dijon's versatility goes far beyond its multiple uses as a condiment. It's the perfect base for Mme Beaupré's homemade vinaigrette (page 21), and if you spread it on your quiche pastry before adding your filling, your dish will have a certain *je ne sais quoi* that no one will be able to identify as mustard.

If you're cooking meat or poultry in a frying pan, stir in a spoonful of Dijon at the end to mix with the pan drippings, followed by a few dollops of crème fraîche (page 30), and you have a delicious, and very easy, sauce. At our house, whether we are in Canada or France, we go through Dijon at a frenetic pace. We even put it on our pasta. Need to cook some fish in a hurry? Coat a salmon or cod fillet with Dijon before throwing it in the oven.

I would advise newbie mustard eaters (*moutardophile* isn't an accepted French expression to describe mustard lovers, but it really ought to be) to start with small dollops of the yellow nectar and then increase the amount when you get used to the spice. A fun tip I learned at family Sunday lunches in France was that if the mustard you are eating *te monte au nez* ("gets in your nose") and makes you want to sneeze, grab your slice of baguette and inhale deeply. The yeast in bread somehow counteracts the spiciness of the mustard. In Burgundy, where the Dijon runs spicy, this tip frequently comes in handy.

My favorite brand of Dijon is Edmond Fallot, made in my adopted hometown of Beaune. I also love Amora and Maille, both local Burgundy brands.

# PASTRY

It has always astounded me how a combination of virtually the same ingredients can come together in so many different ways. Flour, butter, eggs, salt. A liquid of some sort. Sometimes sugar. These items blended together make a myriad of different sweet and savory, earthy and flaky, buttery and light staples. It stands to reason then that the difference lies solely in the technique: temperatures, mixing methods, ratios. There are as many techniques that various bakers swear by as there are types of pie. Here are a few of my favorite tips to help make pastry-making as foolproof as possible. —RW

## BUTTER OR LARD?

A good question whose answer often comes down to personal preference. Butter adds flavor. Lard adds flake. Each used independently works wonderfully, although many people prefer a combination.

Lard is easy to work with and incorporates nicely into flour. Butter has a higher water content, making it a bit more challenging to work into flour, but it also brings that characteristic creamy, irresistible flavor. Unsalted butter is best, as a good-quality one (and you should always use a good-quality one for pastry!) typically has a creamy sweetness. Unsalted also allows you to control the type and amount of salt you add.

Grate butter or lard. We want to keep this important ingredient as cold as possible when making pastry (see next point). Use the large holes in a box grater to make perfectly sized bits of fat that don't require too much fuss to work into your dough, ensuring it stays as cold as possible and you don't overmix.

## KEEP IT CHILL

When making pastry, it is essential that everything remain good and cold. Why? Because it is warmth and kneading that help to form stretchy gluten strands, and with pastry, unlike with bread, we don't want too much of that. We are after a stable dough with a tender flake, not a dense, chewy crumb, when making pies and tarts. If at any point you find the dough warming up too much, pop it back in the fridge for 10–15 minutes to allow the fat to harden again. In the oven, cold fat melts slowly and flaky pockets form. Warm fat melts quickly and flattens.

## BRINGING IT ALL TOGETHER

We've all read the words "do not overmix!" in a recipe. Who else is confused (and a little nervous) about this? When is dough overmixed? What should it look like when it's not overmixed? Each dough recipe will look a wee bit different, yes, but essentially, you want to mix the ingredients until just blended. You will see bits of

butter (this is good) and the dough will hold together well without being too wet or sticky. If your pastry just isn't coming together, add a bit of water—but only a teaspoon or two at a time. A little goes a long way in this case. Too much water will toughen your pastry.

## TAKE FIVE

The resting time for pastry is important. It relaxes the gluten and makes for a tastier, flakier pastry. Are you sensing a theme here? Too much gluten equals tough dough. Never skip this step! A lack of resting can also cause your dough to shrink when baking, ruining your carefully formed pastry crust. Wrap your dough in plastic wrap and pop it in the fridge to rest for at least an hour before using. Remove the dough from the fridge 15 minutes before rolling it out so it's pliable enough that it doesn't crack and break. Once you've rolled out the dough and formed it in the pie plate, return it to the fridge for another 30 minutes while you make your filling and allow the oven to heat.

## GO WITH THE ROLL

When you're ready to roll out your pastry, only lightly flour the surface you are working on. Too much flour will—you guessed it!—make your dough tough. Use a gentle touch here. Most pastries will not tolerate a re-roll, so plan out any cuts or shaping carefully. When your pastry is ready to go into the pie plate, roll it around your rolling pin, then unroll it carefully into the plate, leaving a little extra at the top to allow for a bit of natural shrinkage. Roll out a galette pastry a bit thinner than you would a pie crust. With a galette, you won't be able to pre-bake the crust, because it needs to remain pliable and soft enough to fold over top of the filling. Rolling it a bit thinner will allow it to bake all the way through.

## BLIND BAKING

Blind baking is when you pre-bake the crust prior to adding any filling, then bake again with the filling in place. It is especially important to do this when baking something custardy or that contains quite a bit of liquid, such as fruit pies. Blind baking ensures the bottom of the crust is not left raw and doughy, but has the same warm flake as the rest of the pie. It is an extra step, yes, but undeniably worth it. To blind bake, form your pastry in the pie plate. Cover with parchment paper and fill the pastry shell with 1–2 cups of dried beans (reserve these beans for future baking projects, not for eating!) or baking beads, which you can find at most kitchen stores. Make sure the entire bottom surface of the plate is filled. This allows the pastry to stay flat and not puff up while baking. Blind bake your pastry at a higher heat than you would use to bake the final pie. Baking quickly at the higher temperature helps prevent too much shrinkage.

## THE FINAL BAKE

Get to know your oven! Know its hot spots and temperature accuracy. It's not a bad idea to have an oven thermometer on hand, as different ovens can vary by several degrees in temperature. If your pastry is getting too brown on the top, feel free to cover it lightly with aluminum foil.

# Pâte Sablée

**MAKES ONE (10-INCH) TART CRUST**

This is a shortbread-type pastry that is buttery and crumbly. It's perfect for sweet tarts such as lemon tart (page 199).

Pour the flour into a large bowl. Add the salt, then grate the cold butter over top and cut it in with a pastry cutter until you have a crumbly consistency with some visible little lumps of butter. Make a well in the center and add the sugar, baking powder, egg, and vanilla. Using your fingertips, work the ingredients together just until they come together in a ball.

Set the ball on a lightly floured work surface and, using your hands, work the ingredients together to distribute the butter evenly. Don't overwork the dough, but do blend it well. Spend no more than a minute or two on this step.

Wrap the dough in plastic wrap, flatten it into a thick disk, and give it a good rest in the fridge for a few hours. Once you start shaping the dough, if you find it is cracking and breaking, allow it to rest at room temperature for a few minutes, so it's more pliable. Pâte sablée can be frozen for up to 3 months. Thaw in the fridge overnight before using.

1 cup all-purpose flour

¼ tsp kosher salt

½ cup cold unsalted butter

½ cup granulated sugar

½ tsp baking powder

1 large egg

½ tsp pure vanilla extract

---

# Basic Pastry

**MAKES TWO (10-INCH) CRUSTS**

This flaky, tender basic pastry recipe can be used for sweet or savory pies, tarts, and galettes. To make a sweet pastry, use the sugar; to make a savory pastry, omit the sugar. It's that easy!

In a large bowl, whisk together the flour, sugar (if using), and salt.

Using the large holes in a box grater, grate the butter (or lard) over top of the flour mixture and use a pastry cutter to cut it in.

Add the egg yolk and drizzle in the milk while stirring with a wooden spoon until the dough just starts to stick together. Turn out onto a lightly floured surface and pull the dough together into a ball until all the ingredients are incorporated and stick together. You will see bits of butter (or lard). That's good. Flatten the dough ball lightly with the palm of your hand, wrap in plastic wrap, and let rest in the fridge for at least 3 hours. The dough can be frozen at this point for up to 3 months. Allow it to thaw in the fridge overnight before using.

1½ cups all-purpose flour

1 Tbsp granulated sugar

½ tsp kosher salt

½ cup + 3 Tbsp cold butter or pure lard (or a mix of both)

1 large egg yolk, lightly beaten

3 Tbsp whole milk

# Marie's French Pastry

**MAKES TWO (10-INCH) CRUSTS**

My baking life improved exponentially when I learned a simple and versatile pastry recipe from my friend Marie. When she discovered I bought my pastry from the store she looked at me askance and told me that, *de toute façon*, store-bought pastry could never be even half as good as homemade pastry and that she was going to teach me how to make my own homemade pastry right then and there.

She threw some ingredients into a food processor, mixed them up, and that was it. We had just made pastry. After that day I was off and running. This pastry can be used for many fruit tarts (even though it doesn't contain any sugar) and quiches, and it's hard to express how much I still appreciate Marie's gift of this pastry to me. Now it's time for me to pass it on to you.

2 cups all-purpose flour

1 cup cold butter, cubed

1 tsp sea salt

⅓ cup cold water

Place the flour, butter, and salt in a food processor fitted with the steel blade. Blend until the ingredients are incorporated but you can still see pea-sized bits of butter.

With the processor running, drizzle in the water, watching as the dough comes together and starts to form a ball, about 30 seconds.

If the dough is too dry, add more cold water, 1 Tbsp at a time, until the dough sticks when pinched and is pulling away from the bowl. If it seems too sticky, add more flour, about 2 tsp at a time.

Remove the dough from the bowl, wrap in plastic wrap, and press lightly into a disk. Refrigerate for at least 1 hour before using. At this point, the dough can be frozen for up to 3 months.

Allow it to thaw in the fridge overnight before using.

# A GUIDE TO FRENCH MEALTIMES

Breakfast is not actually an important meal in France. Most days, a good coffee suffices. Occasionally it might be accompanied by a pastry from the local *boulangerie*, but that's about it. Lunch and dinner are the big meals of the day, and generally lunch tends to be the main meal and dinner is a bit lighter.

Meal times are regimented compared to North America, and there is little or no snacking between meals. I have come across many the hapless tourist in France who is desperate to eat but dismayed to find all the restaurants closed at four o'clock in the afternoon. As for me, I love having specific moments in the day carved out to sit down and have a proper meal. I find it gives us an enjoyable and healthy daily ritual.

Breakfast is whenever people get up before noon. Lunch is from noon to two. Children enjoy a *goûter* (see page 43) after school, between four and five o'clock. Dinner is from seven o'clock (at the *very* earliest) to ten o'clock.

Visitors to France are often befuddled by the format of French meals. The information here generally pertains to meals in a restaurant, or when you are either hosting or being hosted, although schoolchildren in France eat a four-course meal every day at school in the *cantine*.

When my family came to visit me in Burgundy they would often think that the starter course (called the *entrée* in France, which can be confusing to North Americans) was the main course. They would serve themselves several times, then blanch in horror when the main course, often a hearty coq au vin or boeuf bourguignon, was brought to the table. I warned them ahead of time, but they didn't seem to believe me. They eventually learned that French meals are all about pacing oneself, so here's a cheat sheet on what to expect.

---

APÉRITIF Usually a drink of kir, champagne, or crémant and some gougères, pâté, or other small, salty snack prior to the meal to *ouvrir l'appétit* (literally, "to open your appetite"), as the French like to say.

ENTRÉE This is your first course. It can be a salad, a terrine, a dozen escargots, some charcuterie, or any number of things to whet your appetite.

PLAT PRINCIPAL This is your main course. It is more substantial and could be a poulet Gaston Gérard, a lovely poached fish, or a roasted leg of lamb with herbes de Provence.

**FROMAGE** Next is the cheese course. Yes, there is an entire course just for cheese—one of the many reasons I fell head over heels for France. Expect a mind-blowing cheese board that you generally serve yourself from. The French tend to take tiny slices, but you can do whatever you want (wink, wink).

**DESSERT** No French meal would be complete without a wee bit of sweetness at the end. Mousse au chocolat, a wonderful homemade cake, or a stunning pastry picked up at a favorite pâtisserie… Yum.

**CAFÉ** It is customary to signal the end of a meal with a shot of espresso.

There you have it! Another important point is that the French are leisurely with the pace of their meals. Some North Americans initially think it's rude that waiters don't come to check on them very often and bring out their food at a far slower pace than back home.

In France, it's the opposite. Rushing customers along would be considered extremely impolite, and it is assumed that everyone wants to take time to linger over their meals. A Sunday lunch in Burgundy usually spans between four and six hours (often longer). That's the difference between eating to live and living to eat.

One of the huge differences between North American and French eating habits concerns snacking. As I mentioned, the French traditionally take time with their meals (an hour-and-a-half to two-hour break at midday to eat lunch is *de rigueur* for many people). As a result, they rarely snack. My French family and friends find it bizarre how we North Americans graze all day long. In their eyes, we eat constantly.

The French have three main meals a day, but there's a fourth meal that has a special status: *le goûter*. This is the after-school snack beloved by schoolchildren all over France, as well as the parents of said schoolchildren, who experience a low blood sugar moment that coincides with the time when *les enfants* burst through the door, hungry and eager to recount the joys and tragedies of their day.

The *goûter* traditionally happens between four and five o'clock and usually consists of something small like a yogurt and some fruit, or my favorite, a few pieces of chocolate inside a sliced piece of baguette (page 53), or a few freshly baked madeleines (the specialty of my friend Marie; page 51). Something a little bit sweet and a big bit satisfying—the perfect pick-me-up for the mid-afternoon doldrums, to get you through to dinner.

Start your own *goûter* tradition with the recipes in this chapter and enjoy a well-deserved pause in your day.

# GOÛTER

# CHOCOLATE BISCUITS WITH MÉMÉ

## MAKES ABOUT 25 SMALL BISCUITS

We were so lucky that Franck's grandmother, known affectionately as Mémé, moved to Beaune the same year that we did. It was such a wonderful opportunity for our daughters Charlotte and Camille to get to know their legendary great-grandmother. She lived in an independent living facility right near the girls' school, and we would often pop by to visit her. I am so grateful for the time the girls had with her, because she passed away five days before our third daughter, Clémentine, was born.

Mémé would always keep her apartment stocked with packages of Les Biscuits Prince for the girls' *goûter*. They were one of the girls' favorite after-school treats: two malted biscuits with a chocolate ganache middle.

Rebecca has created an even more delicious version. A tip from Charlotte and Camille: these are best when dipped in steaming hot chocolate.

½ cup old-fashioned rolled oats

1½ cups whole grain spelt flour

2 Tbsp brown sugar

1 tsp baking powder

½ tsp kosher salt

¼ cup lard, cold and cut into 1-inch pieces

2 Tbsp cold butter, diced

⅓ cup whipping cream

1 cup bittersweet or semisweet chocolate chips

1 Tbsp whipping cream

---

Heat the oven to 400°F. Line two sheet pans with parchment paper.

Place the oats in a food processor and pulse several times until the oats are broken down a bit. Add the flour, sugar, baking powder, and salt, and process until well blended, about 15 seconds.

Add the lard and pulse a few times until well incorporated. Add the butter and repeat. Pour in the cream and process until the dough is well blended and sticks together when you pinch it between your fingers, 30–60 seconds.

Dump the dough onto a lightly floured surface. Knead it with your hands for a minute or so, then press it into a disk. Using a lightly floured rolling pin, roll out the dough to about ¼-inch thickness.

Using a cookie cutter or glass (about 2¼ inches in diameter), cut out rounds of dough and place them on the prepared baking sheets. Place one pan on the top rack of the oven, and the other on the bottom.

Bake until lightly golden with faintly browning edges, 10–15 minutes. Rotate the pans and switch their rack positions halfway through to ensure even cooking. Once baked, transfer to a cooling rack to cool completely.

Place the chocolate chips and cream in a glass or metal bowl. Set the bowl inside a pot one-third filled with water and bring the water to a simmer over medium heat. Stir well until the chocolate chips have almost completely melted. Remove from the heat and stir until the chocolate is smooth.

Using an offset spatula, frost the biscuits with chocolate. Refrigerate for 10 minutes to allow the chocolate to set.

---

*Spelt flour is preferred in this recipe, due to its texture and nutty flavor (it also contains more healthy fiber!), but whole wheat flour can be used in a pinch.* —RW

# SUNDAY NIGHT CRÊPES

## SERVES 6

February gets me every time. As my sister Jayne pointed out, February is like the Tuesday of the winter. It's not the beginning like Monday, which is never as bad as you imagine, but it's not anywhere near the end either. I want warmth and sunshine and spring in February, and Burgundy is not exactly the South of France. So, like the French, I settle for crêpes. Luckily there is a tradition in France called La Chandeleur. The origin of La Chandeleur is a tad vague. It supposedly began when a long-ago pope distributed crêpes to the pilgrims in Rome. However, the French have embraced La Chandeleur and its requisite eating of crêpes with fervor, and I am not one to rock the boat when it comes to eating more crêpes.

This traditional Catholic celebration happens on February 2. Crêpes are never needed more than in these bleak depths of early February. It would be a crying shame, however, to limit your crêpes habit to La Chandeleur. They are perfect for *le goûter*, and we try to make them most Sunday nights for dinner during the winter. Here is our recipe: a balm for our souls and hopefully yours as well.

4 cups all-purpose flour

Pinch of sea salt

6 eggs, lightly whisked

⅓ cup light-tasting vegetable oil

4¼ cups whole milk, divided

Butter for cooking

---

In a large bowl, whisk together the flour and salt. Make a hole in the center of the flour mixture and add the eggs and oil. Continue whisking until the eggs are incorporated, but the batter is stiff and lumpy. Slowly add about 1 cup of the milk, continuously whisking gently, until blended.

Pour the rest of the milk in and whisk everything together. Don't overmix.

Pour the batter through a fine-meshed sieve into a pitcher. This step eliminates the lumps without toughening the batter. Cover the pitcher with plastic wrap and place in the fridge to rest for at least 1 hour and up to overnight.

When you're ready to cook, place a crêpe pan over high heat. (If you don't have a crêpe pan, a nonstick sauté pan will do, though a real crêpe pan will make a big difference, as the bottom is completely flat, the pan is designed to heat evenly, and the sides are very low, making the crêpe much easier to flip.)

Add about ¼ tsp butter and swirl to melt. Pour in ¼–½ cup of batter, using just enough to cover the pan. Tilt the pan this way and that to cover the entire pan with batter. When you see bubbles popping in the middle of the crêpe, after 60–90 seconds, loosen the edges of the crêpe with a silicone spatula. Using your fingers, flip it over to cook the other side briefly, 30–60 seconds. When the crêpe has little brown spots all over, it's cooked.

The first crêpe is usually very weird-looking. It is the same with pancakes, and is just an accepted fact when making crêpes!

Keep the cooked crêpes warm under aluminum foil until ready to serve. Fill them with savory fillings such as ham, grated cheese, and crème fraîche, or keep them sweet and simple with berry jam and a squeeze of lemon.

# MARIE'S LEMON MADELEINES

## MAKES 24 MADELEINES

My dear friend Marie would whip these up all the time for the children's *goûter*. Between the two of us we have seven children, and we would usually converge at one or the other's house every day.

Marie would beat the eggs and the sugar together by hand with a fork and remind me that they needed to be beaten for a good long time until the mixture becomes a pale, pale yellow—almost white. Marie clearly has stronger arms than I do, because I need to use a stand mixer to get that pale shade. Many madeleine recipes call for fleur d'oranger, but I've always preferred Marie's recipe, with its bright taste of lemon. I find the tart citrus is a perfect foil to madeleines' buttery richness.

1 scant cup butter

4 eggs, at room temperature

1 cup granulated sugar

2 tsp grated lemon zest

1 tsp vanilla extract

2 cups all-purpose flour

Icing sugar

Set a small pot over medium heat and melt the butter, making sure it doesn't bubble. Remove from the heat and set aside to cool, about 15 minutes.

Using an electric beater or a metal whisk, mix the eggs on high speed (vigorously, if mixing by hand) with the sugar in a medium-sized bowl until pale in color, about 5 minutes.

Add the lemon zest and vanilla, and whisk to combine. Add the flour and whisk until thoroughly mixed. Whisking constantly, drizzle in the melted butter. Whisk until thoroughly mixed. Cover with plastic wrap, pressing down onto the surface of the batter to avoid it drying out, and allow it to rest in the fridge for at least 3 hours and up to 24 hours.

Heat the oven to 430°F. Grease a 24-cavity madeleine pan and set aside. (If you have a 12-cavity pan, bake them in two batches.)

Scoop the batter into the prepared pan, filling each cavity no more than about three-quarters full. Put the pan in the fridge until the oven has reached temperature.

Place the pan in the oven and immediately lower the temperature to 380°F. Bake for about 5 minutes, then lower the temperature to 350°F. Bake until the edges of each madeleine are golden brown and there is a bump in the middle of the cookie, 5–7 minutes. Lowering the temperature in this manner is how you obtain the infamous madeleine bump!

Immediately remove the madeleines from the pan by gently tapping the pan on the counter. Let cool a little on a cooling rack and sprinkle with icing sugar to taste. Madeleines are best served slightly warm on the day they are made.

# CHOCOLATE IN BAGUETTE

This isn't an actual recipe per se as much as an assemblage. Still, this is my favorite *goûter*, and something that was recommended to me by a nutritionist in France (yes, for real). She pointed out that instead of giving my girls processed pastries or store-bought cookies for their *goûter*, it would be far healthier to take a chunk of baguette, cut it in half, and put in a couple of squares of good-quality milk or dark chocolate.

Simple and crazy delicious. I have turned a few friends on to this snack and they have all reported back that it is one of the most satisfying afternoon snacks they have ever had. I know it sounds childish, but trust me, those French schoolchildren are on to something.

# CANNELÉS

## MAKES 16 CANNELÉS

*D'accord, d'accord…* this recipe is neither easy nor quick, but I thought I'd put it in for the more confident cooks or people like me who learn by leaping into things that are way out of their depth (it's a way of life that is, at least, never boring).

Besides, cannelés are one of my favorite treats in France. They originate from the Bordeaux region, so I feel guilty when I confess my love of them to my Burgundian friends. You see, Burgundy and Bordeaux, the two most important wine-making regions of France, are locked in an unspoken rivalry whereby each thinks their wine is far superior.

These small pastries baked in specifically shaped molds are traditionally flavored with rum and vanilla, but Rebecca has substituted the apple-flavored liqueur Calvados (Franck's favorite) in this recipe. I adore their soft and tender custard center and dark, thick caramelized crust. This recipe should be started at least a day prior to baking to allow the batter to rest and develop its flavor. Still, it is 100% worth the work. *Promis.*

2 cups whole milk

3 Tbsp Calvados

1 tsp pure vanilla extract

1 cup granulated sugar

2 eggs

2 egg yolks

½ cup butter, melted and cooled

½ cup all-purpose flour

¼ tsp sea salt

½ cup butter

In a medium-sized saucepan over medium heat, bring the milk to a simmer. Remove from the heat and mix in the Calvados and vanilla. Set aside.

In a large bowl, whisk together the sugar, eggs, and egg yolks. Whisking constantly, drizzle in the melted butter and continue to whisk until combined. Add about one third of the hot milk mixture, whisking constantly to create a custard. Whisk in the flour and salt until combined. Add the rest of the milk mixture and whisk until all the ingredients are well combined and the batter is smooth.

Cover the bowl with plastic wrap and refrigerate for at least 24 hours and up to 4 days. When you are ready to use the batter, whisk it well, for up to 2 minutes, to combine the ingredients again.

When you are ready to bake, heat the oven to 550°F. Place the cannelé molds on a rimmed sheet pan and heat for 3–4 minutes. Meanwhile, melt the ½ cup butter. Generously brush each mold with it, then place the molds in the freezer for 15 minutes.

Line a room-temperature sheet pan with parchment paper.

Transfer the molds to this sheet pan and fill each mold up to ⅜ inch from the top. Bake for 10 minutes, then, without opening the oven door, lower the oven temperature to 375°F. Bake for another 45–50 minutes, rotating the pan 180 degrees at the halfway point. The cannelés should be dark brown on top. Bake them for another 5 minutes if they're not browned.

Remove from the oven and immediately remove the cannelés from the molds. Place them on a cooling rack to cool to room temperature, about 1 hour. Cannelés will keep in an airtight container at room temperature for up to 3 days.

*The best mold to use to obtain the crispy outside and custard-baked inside of the perfect cannelé is a copper mold. Traditionally, a French pastry chef, or pâtissier, would melt beeswax and butter together and brush the copper molds with it. However, plain butter will do. Silicone molds are a perfectly acceptable alternative. —RW*

# HONEY-GLAZED BRIOCHE

## MAKES 8 LARGE BUNS

My husband, Franck, can be bribed with fresh brioche to do pretty much anything. In France, we always buy it at the *boulangerie*, and Franck prefers it over even the most decadent croissant or pain au chocolat.

Rebecca took this brioche idea and ran with it, creating absolutely adorable little knots of honey-glazed brioche that melt in your mouth and are so beautiful you almost can't bring yourself to eat them (but of course you do, because… brioche… just ask Franck). Note that you need to allow several hours for the dough to rise.

### SPONGE

To prepare the sponge, pour the warm milk into the bowl of a heavy-duty stand mixer not yet attached to the mixer. Using a handheld whisk, gently whisk in the egg. Add the yeast, then 1 cup of the flour. Using a rubber spatula, mix until just combined. Pour the remaining 1 cup of flour gently over top of the mixture and let stand for 40–45 minutes. The yeast will begin to activate, cracking the top of the flour.

### DOUGH

To make the dough, add 1 cup of the flour, the sugar, salt, eggs, and vanilla to the sponge (yeast mixture). Attach the bowl to the mixer and, using the dough hook, mix on low speed for about 1 minute, until everything is combined. Add the remaining ½ cup of flour and turn the mixer up to medium speed. Scraping the bowl as needed, mix for 15–20 minutes. If you find the dough is too wet and sticking to the sides of the bowl, add flour, 1–2 Tbsp at a time, until the dough is forming a ball and attaching itself to the dough hook. It should be soft but not sticky by the time you are done.

Next, add the butter bit by bit. The butter should be softened, but not melted or too oily. As you add it, it will look like it will never incorporate into the dough, but give it some time. Continue to mix on medium speed for 5–7 minutes, until the dough is shiny and only slightly sticky and the butter is worked through.

### RISE #1

Grease a medium bowl with a bit of neutral-tasting vegetable oil. Place the dough, which should be ball-shaped by now, inside and cover with lightly oiled plastic wrap. Let stand at room temperature until doubled in size, about 2 hours.

## Sponge

⅓ cup warm milk (about 120°F)

1 large egg, lightly beaten

2¼ tsp active dry yeast

2 cups all-purpose flour, divided

## Dough

1½ cups all-purpose flour, divided, plus a bit extra as needed

⅓ cup granulated sugar

1 tsp kosher salt

4 large eggs, lightly beaten

1 tsp pure vanilla extract

¾ cup butter, softened, cubed

## Egg Wash

1 large egg yolk

1 Tbsp milk

## Honey Glaze

½ cup icing sugar

1 Tbsp liquid honey

1 Tbsp lemon juice

## RISE #2

After the dough has doubled in size, place four fingertips under one side, lift it gently from the base of the bowl, and then let it fall back into the bowl again. Continue to do this around the entire piece of dough, lifting it and letting it fall. It will deflate a bit. Cover the bowl with plastic wrap and place in the fridge for at least 6 hours, or up to overnight, this time. The dough should double in size again.

## TO BAKE

Remove the dough from the fridge and line a sheet pan with parchment paper. Using a bench scraper, divide the dough into 8 equal-sized pieces. Work with one piece of dough at a time, and keep the remainder in the fridge.

Roll each piece into a snake about 12 inches long. Tie the piece into a loose knot, stretching as you need to, then tuck the ends underneath and pinch to seal. Set on the prepared sheet pan, and repeat with the remaining pieces. Cover loosely with lightly oiled plastic wrap and let proof at room temperature for 2 hours. Heat the oven to 350°F. Beat the egg with the milk to make the egg wash. Using a pastry brush, gently brush the surface of each knot.

Bake until the top of the brioche is golden, 20–25 minutes. Remove from the oven and let cool on a cooling rack for 15 minutes.

## GLAZE

While the brioche cools, make the glaze. Whisk together the icing sugar, honey, and lemon juice in a small bowl. Drizzle onto each knot and eat warm!

A main meal in France generally includes a first course—called an *entrée*—that is served after the apértif and before the main course. Entrées tend to be lighter than the main dish. It is also important to French cooks that the entrée harmonize beautifully with the dishes to follow. For example, a lovely salad with goat cheese would be a nice light prologue to a heartier boeuf bourguignon.

# FOR STARTERS

# KIR

Kir is the most commonly served apéritif in Burgundy. Its history is something that Burgundians, particularly those near the town of Dijon, are proud of.

During the Second World War, residents of Burgundy, who were squarely in Occupied France, responded to wartime privation in a typically pugnacious manner by creating an elegant cocktail out of wine that had not been seized by the German invaders.

A kir cocktail is made with one third crème de cassis, or blackcurrant liqueur, and two thirds dry white wine, traditionally an aligoté from the Hautes-Côtes area of the Côte d'Or, where Villers-la-Faye is nestled. Aligoté wine was always considered a lesser wine than the grand chardonnays of Burgundy, so it never interested the Germans.

A Kir Royale is made with local Burgundian crémant—basically champagne but made outside of the geographic borders of Champagne. The Germans weren't interested in that either.

Both cocktails are named for Félix Kir, a Catholic priest (and, as Burgundians will proudly tell you, a legendary womanizer) and decorated member of the French Resistance. When German soldiers marched into Dijon in 1940, Kir remained in the city, helping more than 4,000 prisoners of war escape from a nearby camp. Legend has it that when the occupying German forces confiscated Burgundy's iconic red wines, Kir defiantly devised his namesake cocktail. He combined the available dry white wine, aligoté, with local blackcurrant liqueur from the Hautes-Côtes.

Franck's grandmother Mémé, who lived to the ripe age of ninety-seven, always swore that kir was the reason she enjoyed a lifetime of almost perfect health. She believed it helped keep her cheerful and prevented arthritis. She knew I loved kir almost as much as she did, and we would often toast each other with our kirs and a complicitous wink.

# FRANCK'S CHEESE GOUGÈRES

**MAKES ABOUT 30**

Let's just get something straight. My husband makes the best gougères I have ever tasted. Before him, his grandmother Mémé made the best gougères I had ever tasted, and she was the one who taught Franck. Mémé was the Queen of Gougères in the family, and Franck is now the King of Gougères.

Gougères are typically Burgundian and are often served with kir as part of the apéritif. The two are a truly sublime combination. At our wedding we had what is called a *vin d'honneur* between the church ceremony and reception, where everyone joined in countless toasts with a garnet glass of kir in one hand and a warm, airy gougère in the other.

Even if I'm furious with Franck (we're both fiery personalities, so it happens), I can't help but fall in love with him all over again when I smell the buttery scent of gougères wafting from our oven.

At family events, Franck is always assigned gougères—who doesn't like a pillowy, cheese-spiked puff? They are not complicated, and they do not use any unusual ingredients, but they do take a certain *coup de main* to know when they are ready to bake. This is a great recipe to experiment with, and when you pull that perfectly puffed gougère out of the oven, it will all be worth it. *Promis.*

6 Tbsp butter

¾ tsp sea salt

¼ tsp freshly grated nutmeg

1¼ cups all-purpose flour

4 large eggs

1½ cups grated Gruyère or Emmenthal cheese

Sesame seeds (optional)

Heat the oven to 400°F. Line two large rimmed sheet pans with parchment paper and set aside.

In a medium pot over high heat, bring 1 cup of water, the butter, salt, and nutmeg to a boil.

Remove from the heat and pour in the flour. Stir vigorously with a wooden spoon until well incorporated. Return the pot to medium-low heat and stir constantly until the mixture forms an elastic-like ball, about 2 minutes.

Place the ball of dough in a large bowl. Add the eggs, one at a time, stirring to incorporate well after each addition. Using your hands, work the grated cheese into the dough.

Using either a spoon or a pastry bag fitted with a large round tip, dollop a tablespoon of dough onto the prepared sheet pan, leaving 1 inch between each dollop. Sprinkle with sesame seeds (if using).

Cook until golden brown and a gougère sounds hollow when tapped on its top, 16–18 minutes. Watch them carefully and do not overcook.

Cool on the pan for 10 minutes before serving.

# CLASSIC FRENCH PISSALADIÈRE

## SERVES 6–8

This recipe hails from Provence, a few hours south of Burgundy. Some of Franck's family moved down to the Ventoux area of Provence, and it was on a family trip to visit them that I first tasted a pissaladière. We had it for a starter for lunch, and I discovered, much to my surprise, that I loved the salty, briny bite of anchovies that form the criss-cross pattern across this gorgeous tart.

Pissaladière will forever taste to me like the South of France on a plate: the shimmering ocean, the ripe tomatoes straight from the vine, and the firm bite of black, shiny niçoise olives from the gnarled olive trees. I love pissaladière warm or straight-out-of-the-fridge cold. With a big green salad, it's one of my favorite meals.

2 Tbsp butter

1 Tbsp olive oil

4 large sweet onions, thinly sliced

2 garlic cloves, minced

2 tsp brown sugar

2 Tbsp balsamic vinegar

2 Tbsp dry white wine

1 Tbsp fresh thyme leaves, divided

1 recipe Marie's French Pastry (page 39) or 1 (10- x 17-inch) sheet of store-bought puff pastry

1 egg yolk

20–24 anchovy fillets, drained and rinsed

8–10 niçoise olives, halved lengthwise (kalamata olives work, too)

Heat a large sauté pan over medium heat and melt the butter. Add the oil and stir to combine. Add the onions and cook, stirring constantly, until they are softened, 25 minutes. Add the garlic, brown sugar, balsamic, and wine and continue to cook, stirring, until the onions are browned and sticky and the liquid has all disappeared, 10–15 minutes. Season with 1½ tsp of the thyme and some sea salt and pepper, and set aside to cool for 10 minutes.

Heat the oven to 425°F. Line a large rimmed sheet pan with parchment paper.

Roll out the pastry to a 10- x 17-inch rectangle that's ⅛-inch thick. Lay it gently on the prepared sheet pan. (If you are using store-bought puff pastry, note that it comes in a variety of sizes, so you may need to press two pieces together here to fit your sheet pan.) Using a sharp knife, lightly score the pastry around the entire perimeter, leaving a 1-inch border on all sides. Using a fork, poke holes all over the crust so it doesn't puff up. Mix the egg yolk with 1 tsp of water and brush over only the border of the crust.

Bake the crust until slightly browned, 10–12 minutes.

Spread the onions evenly over the crust, inside the border. Place the anchovy fillets over the onions to make diamonds and place an olive half inside each diamond.

Return to the oven for 15 minutes, just until heated through and well browned. Sprinkle with the remaining 1½ tsp thyme. Serve hot, at room temperature, or even cold.

*When caramelizing onions, low and slow is the secret. You want to cook them over just enough heat to cara- melize and brown. Just when you think they're done, keep going! A good 40–50 minutes is required to properly caramelize onions. Because they're a bit high maintenance, double the batch and keep the extra in the fridge for a week. As for anchovies, be sure to buy the highest quality possible and taste them before placing them on the pissaladière. Some are extremely salty and require a rinse before using. —RW*

# CELERIAC REMOULADE

I didn't discover celeriac, aka celery root, until I traveled to France for my exchange year when I was eighteen. It wasn't until three or four years later that I realized that the rather uninspiring stalks of celery that we used to make "ants on a log" at the potlucks of my youth and celeriac belonged *to the same plant*. I know, right?

Let's be frank here, the celery root is not blessed in the beauty department. It's basically a big, bumpy, brownish lump. I think one of the reasons it's not popular in North America is that it's pretty much impossible to "glow up" in any way, shape, or form. What it lacks in exterior beauty, however, it more than makes up for in its fresh, woodsy flavor. One of the most traditional ways of eating celeriac in France is shredded celeriac salad, which my girls often ate at lunch in the school cafeteria in France. Much to my initial surprise, they loved it and asked me to make it at home.

To thank France for bringing celeriac into my life, I'm now going to bring it into yours.

1 cup Lemon Aioli (page 29) or quality mayonnaise

2–4 Tbsp Dijon mustard

2 tsp grated lemon zest

2 Tbsp lemon juice

2¼ lb celery root

---

Prepare the dressing first, as celeriac discolors quickly once grated. In a small bowl or measuring cup, whisk together the mayonnaise (or aioli), Dijon to taste (start with 2 Tbsp and work your way up), lemon zest, and lemon juice. Set aside.

Using a sharp knife, carefully cut the top and bottom off the celeriac. Stand it on one of the now-flat ends and use a sharp knife to cut off the bark-like exterior skin. Cut the celeriac into quarters and grate them into matchstick-sized pieces on a box grater, in a food processor, or with a mandoline.

In a large bowl, mix together the celeriac and dressing. Season with sea salt and pepper, cover, and put in the fridge for an hour or two before serving.

---

*This is a classic recipe, and I love its simplicity! You may feel as though you have too much dressing when you first toss the salad. However, celeriac is very absorbent and will soak up the dressing before you know it. Don't be afraid to use it all. Enjoy its simple nature for sure, but if you'd like to add to the salad, a grated carrot, green apple, or some toasted seeds or nuts are a great addition.* —RW

# RADISHES WITH BUTTER AND SALT

### SERVES 2–4

I adore this simple combination of ingredients and eat it often as either an entrée to a larger meal or a light meal on its own (in France, pacing oneself is a matter of survival!). Fresh red radishes with high-quality butter and fleur de sel are one of those simple yet surprisingly perfect combinations that opened my eyes to an entirely new way of eating in France.

1 large bunch fresh radishes, greens removed

⅓ cup unsalted butter, cold

Fleur de sel

Arrange the radishes (if you want to cut them all fancy into flowers, go for it), butter, and salt on a platter. To eat, scrape up a bit of butter with a knife and sprinkle on some fleur de sel as desired.

# GERMAIN REUNION SALAD

**SERVES 4**

I discovered this odd-sounding yet delicious salad during a weekend birthday celebration for Franck's grandfather, Papy Albert. The extended family spent the weekend in a massive stone farmhouse in the Beaujolais hills and passed most of the time eating, drinking, and playing *pétanque*.

Clémentine was only six months old, and her favorite spot during the festivities was right in the middle of the huge L-shaped trestle table, where she sat chewing a spoon among the wine bottles and baskets of baguette slices. She was our de facto table centerpiece during all our multi-hour family meals. When I say children are welcome everywhere in France, I mean it.

Franck's cousin brought this salad to the party. Although I was initially skeptical of the list of ingredients, I was blown away by its fresh combination of flavors. I've had friends make this with watermelon, apricots, and plums, and they have reported back that it's equally delicious. You can serve it either in a big salad bowl for a potluck-style offering or in cute little glass bowls or cups to make it look a bit more *élégante*. A garnish of mint makes it a wee bit fancier.

1 English cucumber, seeds removed, chopped

1 cantaloupe, seeds removed, and flesh chopped or scooped out in balls

2 cups cherry tomatoes, halved

1 recipe Mme Beaupré's Homemade Vinaigrette (page 21)

1⅓ cups crumbled feta cheese

Few sprigs fresh mint

---

In a large bowl, thoroughly toss the cucumbers, melons, and tomatoes with the vinaigrette until coated. Season with sea salt and pepper.

Crumble the feta over top and mix gently to combine. Snip the mint over top and serve.

# NEW YEAR'S OYSTERS ON THE SHELL
## with Green Apple Mignonette

MAKES 24 OYSTERS AND ½ CUP MIGNONETTE

I ate, or rather slurped, my first raw oyster in Paris. Let me tell you, eating your first raw oyster is a major rite of passage. It wasn't until I moved to Paris with Franck to go to the Sorbonne for a year that I realized just how instrumental raw oysters are at French Christmas and New Year's celebrations. Around mid-December, weather-worn fisher-types began setting up stalls in the markets and sometimes just on the street corners, selling wooden boxes of oysters by the dozen all over Paris.

I was first presented with a platter of raw ones at a dinner at a friend's house in Montmartre. Initially I hesitated, but when I saw everyone else squeezing fresh lemon juice on top and slurping them down with glee, I decided to jump into the fray. Carpe diem, etc. Franck knew I had my doubts, so he prepared my first oyster for me, selecting a small one to get me started. He spread butter on my baguette slice, then squeezed fresh lemon juice on it just before passing it over to me. I tipped the oyster into my mouth and swallowed it whole. It tasted briny and mysterious like the sea. From that moment on, I slurped oysters just like any French person.

2½ Tbsp finely minced green apple (about ¼ small apple)

1 small shallot, finely minced (about 1 Tbsp)

¼ tsp granulated sugar

¼ tsp sea salt

½ cup white wine vinegar or champagne vinegar

1½ tsp lemon juice

24 fresh, small, sweet oysters such as Miyagi or Kusshi

To make the mignonette, combine the apple, shallot, sugar, salt, vinegar, and lemon juice in a small bowl. Cover with plastic wrap and let sit in the fridge for at least 20 minutes and up to 1 hour.

Fill a deep, wide platter with crushed ice. Shuck the oysters and place them on the half-shell on the ice. Serve with a dish of mignonette. Add about ¼ tsp mignonette to each oyster before slurping back with pleasure.

# WEDDING FRENCH ONION SOUP

### SERVES 6

Is there anything more French than French onion soup? I think not, and few people do it better than the Burgundians. It happens to be exactly what I feel like when the thermometer plummets, whether I'm in the icy fog of Burgundy or the sleeting rain of the Pacific Northwest.

French onion soup has an important role to play in traditional French weddings. I didn't know this until Franck and I began the meal planning (a BIG deal) for our wedding reception in a wine cellar in Nuits-Saint-Georges. He and his family were insistent that we serve bowls of French onion soup in the wee hours of the morning to our wedding guests. French onion soup, it turned out, was crucial to everyone getting their second wind and ensuring the wedding was a success. In Burgundy, a wedding that doesn't go until dawn is considered a rather paltry affair.

As it turns out, at three o'clock in the morning I was more than happy to down a comforting bowl of this hot, oniony broth to further fuel my dancing and revelry. In my experience, French onion soup tastes best when you are wearing your wedding dress (seriously, try it if you have one kicking around), but it is plenty delicious the rest of the time too.

---

In a large saucepan over medium-low heat, melt 2 Tbsp of the butter and the oil. Add the onions and season with sea salt and pepper. Cook, stirring occasionally, until the onions are soft, golden brown, and caramelized, about 50 minutes. Lower the heat if the onions are getting too brown.

Add the wine to the onions and increase the heat to high. Cook, stirring occasionally, until the liquid has reduced a bit, about 10 minutes.

Add the broth, keeping the temperature high. Add the thyme and bay leaves (it helps to tie the sprigs and leaves together with a little twine, like a bouquet garni, page 19). Give it all a stir to combine.

Bring to a boil then turn down the heat to a simmer, and cook, uncovered, until the broth is deep and flavorful, about 30 minutes. Remove from the heat and whisk in 2 Tbsp of the butter and the sherry. Remove the thyme and bay leaves, taste, and season with sea salt and pepper. Cover to keep warm.

Heat the oven to broil. Place the baguette slices on a large parchment-lined baking sheet and spread the top with the remaining 2 Tbsp of butter. Broil until nicely browned and crisped, 4–6 minutes. Rub each toast with the halved garlic clove and set aside.

Place six large ramekins or ovenproof bowls on a large baking sheet. Ladle soup into each one. Top each bowl with two slices of toast. Divide the cheese among the bowls, covering the bread. Carefully transfer the baking sheet to the oven and broil until the cheese is melted and browned, 6–8 minutes. Serve immediately.

6 Tbsp butter, divided

1 Tbsp vegetable oil

5 medium-sized sweet onions, halved and thinly sliced

1½ cups dry white wine

6 cups Beef Stock (page 25 or store-bought)

10 sprigs thyme

2 bay leaves

1 Tbsp dry sherry

1 best-quality baguette, sliced diagonally into 12 pieces

1 garlic clove, peeled and halved

4 oz Gruyère cheese, grated (about 1 cup)

---

*If you don't have ovenproof bowls, sprinkle cheese on top of the baguette slices after rubbing them with garlic and return to the oven until the cheese is bubbly and brown, 4–6 minutes. Top each bowl of soup with cheesy toast and serve.—RW*

# ARTICHOKE AND ASPARAGUS TART

## SERVES 6–8

Artichokes and asparagus are two vegetables that I got to know extremely well in France. I knew they existed before I arrived in Burgundy, but my opinions about them were noncommittal at best. All that changed (like so many things… like almost *everything*) during my first twelve months.

My first host mother taught me how to eat freshly steamed artichoke leaves with my hands, dipping them into her homemade vinaigrette (page 21) and then scraping off the tender flesh with my front teeth. I was *conquise*, as the French would say.

My second host mother grew white asparagus and bottled up the stalks to eat throughout the winter. Chilled and chubby, white asparagus stalks dipped in homemade mayonnaise spiked with Dijon mustard became one of my favorite lunch or dinner entrées, even in the depths of my first frigid, snowy January in France. They were like a delicious time-travel machine to the spring.

This recipe Rebecca created combines these two quintessentially French flavors in a delectable tart. Perfect in spring, of course, but frankly gorgeous any time of year, served with a fresh tomato and herb salad.

---

Heat the oven to 450°F. Line a large rimmed sheet pan with parchment paper.

Lay the asparagus on the pan and drizzle with 1 Tbsp of the oil. Season with sea salt and pepper. Roast until just tender, about 6 minutes.

Wash the leeks well and drain completely. Heat a large sauté pan over medium heat. Melt the butter with the remaining 1 Tbsp oil. Add the leeks and cook, stirring constantly, until softened, about 10 minutes. Add the garlic and cook until fragrant, another 2 minutes. Add the wine and scrape up any bits at the bottom of the pan. Add the artichoke hearts and cook until the wine has evaporated, 3–5 minutes. Remove from the heat, stir in the thyme and rosemary, season with sea salt and pepper, and set aside.

Roll out the pastry to a 10- x 17-inch rectangle that's ⅛-inch thick. Lay the pastry gently onto the prepared sheet pan. (If you are using store-bought puff pastry, note that it comes in a variety of sizes, so you may need to press two pieces together here to fit your sheet pan.) Lightly score a line around the inside, about 1 inch from the edge, to form a border. Poke holes with a fork throughout the base of the pastry so it doesn't puff up.

Bake until the crust is slightly browned, 7–10 minutes. If necessary, press down on the dough inside of the border with a fork so it doesn't puff up too much. You want the border to remain slightly higher than the inside. Remove from the oven.

CONTINUED ON PAGE 83.

1 lb asparagus, trimmed

2 Tbsp olive oil, divided

1 Tbsp butter

2 large leeks, chopped into ¼-inch rounds, white and light-green parts only

2 cloves garlic, minced

3 Tbsp dry white wine

1 (6 oz) jar marinated artichoke hearts, drained and chopped

2 tsp thyme leaves, minced

1 tsp rosemary leaves, minced

1 recipe Marie's French Pastry (page 39) or 1 (10- x 17-inch) sheet of store-bought puff pastry

2 whole eggs

1 egg, divided

⅓ cup whipping cream

¼ tsp sea salt

¼ tsp grated nutmeg

1 cup grated Gruyère or Emmenthal cheese

1 Tbsp chopped chives

Lemon wedges for serving

Whisk the 2 whole eggs and 1 egg white with the cream. Season with the ¼ tsp salt, the nutmeg, and some pepper.

Whisk the remaining yolk with 1 tsp of cold water and brush only the border of the crust with it.

Spread the leek mixture evenly over the base of the crust, inside the border. Top with about ½ cup of the cheese. Carefully pour the egg mixture over the whole thing, ensuring you get into all the nooks and crannies. Top with the asparagus spears, laid out side by side. Sprinkle with the remaining ½ cup cheese.

Bake until the crust is puffed and toasty brown and the cheese is bubbling, 15–20 minutes. Top with the chives. Let rest for 5 minutes before cutting.

Serve with lemon wedges.

*Not all recipes need to be drawn out and time-consuming, so as mentioned above, feel free to use store-bought pastry and jarred marinated artichoke hearts. However, if you'd like to make your own artichoke hearts—a great thing to have in the fridge, in any case—simply combine a 14 oz jar of plain artichoke hearts with 2 tsp finely minced garlic, 1 tsp grated lemon zest, ½ tsp chili flakes, ¼ cup mild-flavored olive oil, 2 Tbsp lemon juice, and some salt and pepper. Let sit for at least 2 hours before using.—RW*

# POTATO LEEK SOUP

## SERVES 6

In the winter in Burgundy it's traditional to eat a lot of soup. It's enjoyed almost every night before dinner, or as dinner with some cheese or some fruit afterward. Between November and March we usually make a pot of soup with whatever we have kicking around in the fridge every three or four days. Not only are soups warm and comforting winter fare, but they also happen to be excellent at filling all of us up, children and adults alike, with nutritious vegetables. One of my very favorite winter soups is a silky combination of potato and leek, both quintessential French country ingredients.

If you can make this with a homemade chicken or vegetable stock, it will taste even better, but I have been known to use a bouillon cube or a packaged stock when pressed for time. It's still delicious, and the delicate flavor of the leeks and its pale color mean it is refined enough to do double-duty at a dinner party, with a swirl of homemade crème fraîche (page 30) for that special touch.

2 Tbsp butter

4 large leeks, white and light-green parts roughly chopped and thoroughly rinsed

2 medium russet potatoes, peeled and quartered

2 bay leaves

4 cups Chicken Stock or Vegetable Broth (page 26)

1 cup half-and-half cream

2 Tbsp minced chives

Extra virgin olive oil for drizzling (optional)

In a large heavy-bottomed pot over medium heat, melt the butter and add the leeks. Cook, stirring, until softened, 10–12 minutes.

Add the potatoes, bay leaves, and stock and season lightly with sea salt and pepper. Bring to a boil, turn down the heat to a simmer, and cook until the potatoes are very tender, about 15 minutes. Remove from the heat and let cool for 15 minutes. Discard the bay leaves.

Stir in the cream. Using an immersion or stand blender, blend the soup until smooth, 2–3 minutes. If you use a stand blender, vent the lid to allow any residue steam to escape. You may also have to work in batches.

Return the soup to the pot and warm it over low heat, stirring constantly to avoid sticking. Taste and adjust seasoning if needed.

Garnish with chives and drizzle with olive oil.

*Feel free to use whole milk if you prefer, though cream is definitely recommended. And play with the garnish: instead of the chives listed in the recipe, try fresh herbs, such as parsley, or crumbled cheese.*

*Soup is typically thought of as a cooler weather meal; however, potato leek soup is also referred to as vichyssoise, which is traditionally served cold. Do what you like here. Serve it cold if you wish, or warm it up for those cooler days. —RW*

# SALMON RILLETTES

### SERVES 4–6

In France, rillettes are usually made of duck, rabbit, or pork. The meat is salted and cooked in fat until it flakes apart. It's then served at room temperature or slightly chilled, swiped over a slice of baguette. Rillettes melt in your mouth, but unfortunately, they are not easy to find in stores in North America. Luckily, they're easy to make at home.

When I suggested a rillettes recipe, Rebecca had the genius idea of rillettes made of salmon. Wild salmon is plentiful here on our island in the Pacific Northwest and I grew up ocean fishing in my dad's yellow boat, so this was ideal as far as I was concerned. These are not only lighter than traditional rillettes but also prettier—and every bit as tasty.

---

Place a medium pot over high heat. Add the wine, ½ cup water, ½ the shallot, the lemon slice, and a pinch of salt. Bring to a boil. Turn down the heat to a simmer, add the salmon fillet, cover, and cook for 5–10 minutes, depending on thickness. Remove from the heat and set aside, covered, for 10 minutes. Transfer the salmon to a plate and discard the cooking liquid. Let the salmon cool, covered, in the fridge for at least 20 minutes.

Finely mince the remaining ½ shallot. Rinse it in cold water and dry between two paper towels.

In a medium bowl, beat the butter with a fork until well softened and easy to spread. Add the shallot, scallions, capers, lemon zest, lemon juice, aioli (or mayonnaise), and Dijon. Stir until well combined. Fold in the lox.

Remove the cooked salmon from the fridge, cut it into bite-sized pieces, and gently stir it into the smoked salmon mixture. Season with pepper and add more lemon juice and salt if needed. (Typically, the lox gives you enough salt, so use your discretion.) Fold in the dill and cilantro.

Cover the bowl with plastic wrap and refrigerate for a few hours, and up to 3 days. Serve with slices of baguette or French bread.

½ cup dry white wine

1 shallot, peeled and halved

Thin slice of lemon

8 oz salmon fillet, skin and bones removed, kept in one piece

2 Tbsp butter, softened

3 scallions, white and light-green parts minced (about ¼ cup)

1 Tbsp capers, rinsed, patted dry, and finely diced

2 tsp grated lemon zest

2 Tbsp lemon juice

¼ cup Lemon Aioli (page 29) or store-bought mayonnaise

2 Tbsp Dijon mustard

¼ lb lox, cut into ½-inch squares

2 Tbsp minced dill

1 Tbsp minced cilantro

Baguette or French Bread (page 159), for serving

# MICHÈLE'S TABBOULEH

## SERVES 4–6

This isn't exactly a French recipe per se, but I wrote about it often in my Grape Series books because Michèle, my mother-in-law, makes a fabulous tabbouleh salad that is just the thing for scorching hot Burgundian days. Most summers around Beaune bring at least one heat wave with them and the temperature can hover around a wilting 100°F. No one feels like eating hot food, so Michèle and most of my family and friends in France enjoy tabbouleh salads frequently in the warmer months.

This recipe shows the North African influence in French cuisine, and also the flexibility of French recipes. Another bonus is that tabbouleh, while often served as an entrée in Burgundy, is essentially a meal in a bowl. You can truly add almost anything to this recipe. I've seen it made with chopped-up hard-boiled eggs, tuna, cubed feta, palm hearts, artichokes, cubed saucisson sec, all varieties of vegetables… It's one of those handy "raid your fridge and cupboards" sort of recipes. Keep experimenting until you find your favorite combination (or three!).

---

Place the cooked couscous in a large salad bowl.

Place the onion in a fine sieve and rinse with warm water. Drain well and add to the couscous. Add the garlic, tomatoes, zucchini, bell pepper, and radishes and toss well. Add the oil and lemon juice and stir to blend. Fold in the herbs.

Season generously with sea salt and pepper. Cover and place in the fridge for at least 1 hour before serving.

4 cups cooked medium or fine couscous

½ small red onion, minced

1 garlic clove, finely minced

1½ cups cherry tomatoes, halved

1 medium fresh green zucchini, cut into ½-inch dice

1 small red bell pepper, cut in ½-inch dice

5 radishes, thinly sliced

¼ cup olive oil

3 Tbsp lemon juice

½ cup minced fresh mint

½ cup minced fresh parsley

# MARIE'S FRENCH TOMATO TART

SERVES 6–8

This recipe is a complete, hands-down winner. My dear friend Marie gave me this recipe, and I make it at least two or three times a month. It uses the magic of Burgundian Dijon mustard to give the tart an extra wee *je ne sais quoi*. Don't skip the Dijon layer: the tart will not taste nearly as scrumptious without it.

Not only is it dead easy, but it also looks gorgeous and tastes delicious. While it's better with summer tomatoes, of course, it can even magically summon flavor from watery grocery store tomatoes in the dead of winter. It's perfect served with a green salad.

1 recipe Marie's French Pastry (page 39)

1 Tbsp Dijon mustard

1 cup grated cheese (Gruyère, Emmenthal, or Comté are best, but your favorite hard cheese will do)

3–4 tomatoes (depending on size), cored and sliced into ¼-inch rounds

Heat the oven to 400° F. Line a large rimmed sheet pan with parchment paper.

On a lightly floured surface, roll out the pastry to ⅛-inch thick. You should have a rectangle measuring about 9 x 12 inches. Rough edges are totally fine. Roll it carefully onto a rolling pin and unroll onto prepared sheet pan. Using a fork, poke holes all over the pastry surface so it doesn't puff up.

Spread the Dijon over the pastry shell, leaving a 1-inch border around the edges, then sprinkle the cheese evenly over top. Lay tomato rounds over the cheese layer so they touch but do not overlap. Season with sea salt and pepper.

Bake until the cheese is bubbly and the crust is brown, 25–35 minutes.

Let rest for 5 minutes before slicing and serving.

# ENDIVE AND APPLE SALAD
## with Gruyère and Walnuts

### SERVES 4–6

This endive salad is one of my favorite things on this earth. Endive (often called chicory here in North America) is grown in northern France and in Belgium. The grocery stores and markets in France are full of these lovely pale green, chubby specimens. I love endives so much I sometimes snack on them like carrots—but this is considered weird everywhere, so that's just me. They have a tender flavor with a satisfyingly bitter kick, the perfect foil to cheese and nuts in a delicious salad.

This salad is best made right before you serve it because endive has an annoying tendency to turn brown quickly (but I will forgive it because it is so delicious).

Line a rimmed sheet pan with parchment paper and set aside.

Place a large skillet over medium-low heat and melt the butter. Once it's melted, add the sugar and stir constantly until it melts as well, 5–7 minutes.

Add the walnuts and salt and stir to thoroughly coat. Spoon the walnuts onto the prepared pan and separate them with two forks to ensure they don't stick together in one big mass. Let cool, 10 minutes.

Core each endive by cutting up from the base in a V shape. Cut each endive in half lengthwise, cut each half into quarters lengthwise, then chop five or six rows to produce chopped leaves.

Place the endives in a large bowl and add the apple. Pour the lemon juice over top and stir well to coat (this prevents everything from turning brown).

Toss with your desired amount of vinaigrette, and mix well. Just before serving, add the cheese and nuts. Toss the salad again and season with sea salt and pepper. Serve immediately.

1 Tbsp butter

¼ cup packed brown sugar

¾ cup toasted walnut halves

½ tsp sea salt

5 medium-sized Belgian endives

1 apple, cored and cut into bite-sized cubes (Granny Smiths are perfect for this salad)

2 Tbsp lemon juice

1 recipe Mme Beaupré's Homemade Vinaigrette (page 21)

7 oz Gruyère cheese, cut into bite-sized cubes

*Gruyère is an oft-used cheese in French cooking. However, it and its close relative Emmenthal are actually from areas in Switzerland with the same names. Both are made from cow's milk and are flavorful and melt easily, making them the perfect ingredient for many creamy, cheesy French recipes. Comté, Gruyère's French cousin, is pretty much the equivalent of Gruyère, but it is often much fuller in flavor (not necessarily a bad thing) and not always as easy to find. If you do find Comté, feel free to use it in place of Gruyère or Emmenthal in any of the recipes in this book.—RW*

# FRESH GREENS WITH LARDONS
## and Fromage de Chèvre

### SERVES 4

A French goat cheese salad is pretty much my perfect meal… or in my top five anyway. I don't think I can actually narrow my favorites down to just one, but I did warn you that I'm a *gourmande*. I remember when one of my host mothers took me to Paris for the first time and treated me to lunch at her favorite lunch spot, Au Pied du Cochon, which specialized in—you guessed it—pig's feet.

Many of the chic Parisian patrons, though, were dining on green salad leaves shimmering in a light vinaigrette, topped with toasted baguette and goat cheese tartines. I wanted *that*, not the gelatinous, breaded pig foot that was placed in front of me. I did manage to eat the pig's foot because I was nothing if not a good guest, but the idea of eating a pig's foot still makes me gag (although Franck loves them), whereas a goat cheese salad is, in my mind, perfection.

½ lb pancetta, thickly sliced and cut into 1¼-inch strips

Mme Beaupré's Homemade Vinaigrette (page 21)

1 baguette

½ lb fresh goat cheese

8–10 cups fresh greens of your choice, washed and torn into bite-sized pieces (butter lettuce or frisée are great, but any light greens work)

2 Tbsp best-quality liquid honey

Heat a large frying pan over medium heat and add the pancetta, stirring frequently until lightly browned and slightly crispy, about 7–10 minutes. Using a slotted spoon, move the pancetta to some paper towel to drain. Keep about 1 Tbsp of the pork fat from the pan. *Voilà!* You've just made lardons. Stir the reserved fat into the vinaigrette.

Heat the oven to broil. Line a baking sheet with parchment paper.

Slice the baguette on the diagonal into eight slices, each ½-inch thick. (You may have extra baguette.) Spread the goat cheese on the baguette slices. Broil until the cheese is a bit melty and the bread is toasty around the edges, 8–10 minutes. Watch closely, as the broil temperature in ovens can vary.

Toss the prepared greens with the vinaigrette and divide between four plates. Season with sea salt and pepper and sprinkle with the lardons. Place two goat cheese toasts on each plate and drizzle the goat cheese with a bit of honey.

*Lardons are small strips or cubes of bacon or any fatty, cured pork. They provide an excellent smoky flavor to many dishes and are used extensively in French cuisine. You will sometimes see them being used for larding, which means threading the little pieces of lardons and sewing them into cuts of meat for roasting or braising. Bacon is a great substitute for pancetta in this recipe.* —RW

# WARM BEET SALAD
## *with Greens and Feta*

### SERVES 6

Shortly after we moved back to France with Charlotte and Camille to restore our 16th-century vinter's cottage, Franck introduced me to the packages of peeled, cooked beets sold at the local grocery store. I demanded to know why he hadn't introduced me to these globular miracles during any of our previous stays in France and of course, he just shrugged. He did not have a satisfactory explanation for this oversight. All of a sudden beet salad became as easy as chopping up the beets inside. Beets began to appear frequently on our lunch table and the girls quickly came to love them as much as we did.

Rebecca has upped the deliciousness of our humble cubed beet salad by caramelizing them and twinning them with green chard and feta. *Oh là là.*

6 medium-sized beets with greens (a mixture of red and golden is nice)

1 bunch Swiss chard

3 Tbsp butter, divided

2 shallots, julienned

2 Tbsp dry white wine

½ cup toasted hazelnuts

¾ lb goat feta cheese, cut into 6 slices

Maple-Dijon Vinaigrette (page 22)

Remove the greens from the beets and chop coarsely, reserving a few small leaves for garnish. Set the greens aside in a large bowl. Remove the large middle ribs from the Swiss chard, coarsely chop, and toss into the bowl with the beet greens. Scrub and peel the beets, then slice them into ¼-inch rounds.

Heat a large sauté pan over low heat and melt 2 Tbsp of the butter. Add the shallots and sauté until softened, 7–10 minutes. Remove the shallots from the pan with a slotted spoon and set aside.

Add the beets to the pan, adding a ½ Tbsp of the remaining butter if needed. Season with sea salt and pepper and sauté the beets, turning them over several times to coat each piece in butter. Place a lid on top to steam the beets, checking in frequently and adjusting the heat so the beets don't get too dry. After about 15 minutes, when the beets are beginning to glaze and become tender, return the shallots to the pan and cook, uncovered, until the beets are tender and the shallots are caramelized, 5 minutes or so. Transfer the beets and shallots to a large plate.

Add the remaining ½ Tbsp butter to the pan and toss in all the greens. Using tongs, turn the greens to coat them with the butter. Add the wine to the pan, cover, and let cook until the greens are just wilted, about 3 minutes. Add a tablespoon or two of water if the greens begin to stick to the pan.

Divide the greens between six plates and top with the beets and shallots. Garnish with the hazelnuts and reserved beet greens and set a slice of feta on the side. Drizzle with the dressing, season with salt, and grind a bit of pepper over the entire dish.

Here we arrive at the heart of the French meal. The main course should be an EVENT. It doesn't necessarily have to look perfect—the beauty of a boeuf bourguignon, for example, is in the eye of the beholder—but it has to smell and taste delicious. The French will often buy a dessert or even an entrée to serve to guests, but a rule of thumb is that if you are going to cook only part of the meal, it should be the main course. The recipes in this section will give you an unbeatable repertoire of delectable main courses that will let you impress without stress.

# THE MAIN EVENT

# ROUTIER TOMATES FARCIES

The best stuffed tomatoes I have ever eaten were at a *routier*, a diner in France frequented by tradespeople and truck drivers. We were in the town of Louhans, looking for a second-hand car shortly after moving to France with our daughters.

One of Franck's old friends, Réné, was a *garagiste* and had offered to help us locate the perfect vehicle. However, that morning we had toured the market, eaten veal brains, and bought a live chicken. . . but we had not looked at a single car. I was more than a bit frustrated by the time Réné led us into his favorite *routier* in Louhans for lunch. However, the divine stuffed tomatoes reconciled me to Réné and our somewhat fruitless day. The meat stuffing was a succulent mix of sausage and beef, infused with the tomatoes' juice. This was all washed down by a surprisingly good house red.

There are two lessons to be gleaned from Réné and my tomates farcies experience. First, if you're in France, find a *routier* to eat lunch in—you will not find a more delicious, authentic experience. Second, as Réné said, "Never confuse what is urgent with what is truly important."

Good tomates farcies are far more valuable than a car any day.

1 lb seasoned sausage meat

1 small onion, minced

2 garlic cloves, minced

1 cup chopped curly parsley

½ tsp kosher salt

1 cup long-grain white rice

6 large, round tomatoes

---

"*Never confuse what is urgent with what is truly important.*"

---

Place the oven rack in the center position and heat the oven to 400°F.

Combine the meat, onion, garlic, and parsley in a medium-sized bowl. Set aside.

Bring 2 cups of water to a boil in a medium-sized saucepan. Add the salt and then the rice. Turn down the heat to medium and boil, uncovered, for 5 minutes. Stir gently once or twice so the rice doesn't stick to the bottom of the pot. Drain through a fine-mesh sieve, rinse with cold water, and drain again. Add the rice to the meat mixture and stir to mix well.

Cut the tops evenly off the tomatoes, keeping the lid, and empty the guts with a spoon. (A small paring knife helps with this.) Discard any of the watery juice. Chop the tomato guts roughly and season with salt and pepper.

Scatter the tomato guts evenly in a 9- x 13-inch baking dish. Place the hollow tomatoes, cut side up, on top of the guts and sprinkle lightly with salt and pepper.

CONTINUED ON PAGE 105.

Divide the meat mixture evenly among the tomatoes and top with the tomato lids. Cover loosely with aluminum foil and bake until the rice and sausage are fully cooked, 35–45 minutes.

Let sit for 10 minutes before serving.

*This is the perfect almost one-dish meal. For the sausage meat, ask your butcher if they will sell you seasoned meat outside of the casing, or you can simply snip the tip off the sausages and squeeze the meat out. Pork, beef, turkey, and chicken all work well for this and best of all, leftovers freeze beautifully.—RW*

# LAURA'S SNOWSTORM LEEK AND GOAT CHEESE QUICHE

### SERVES 6

I find leeks are sadly neglected in North American kitchens, and their silky texture and delicate flavor deserve to be celebrated. Even though every leek I've ever met is full of sand and needs to be thoroughly rinsed, the reward of this quiche is greater than the work involved in making it.

I made this for a group of guests from Brooklyn staying in one of our vacation rentals who had plowed into a snowbank trying to drive from the neighboring village in the middle of a blizzard. A winemaker friend of ours from Villers used his vineyard tractor to rescue them, then brought them to our house to warm up and have lunch. We became firm friends and have remained in touch. They rave about this "snowstorm" quiche I whipped up for lunch.

1 Tbsp butter

4 large leeks, white and light-green parts halved, then sliced into ½-inch slices

3 Tbsp dry white wine

2 tsp fresh thyme leaves

½ recipe Basic Pastry (savory) (page 38)

1 Tbsp Dijon mustard

4 oz creamy goat cheese

1 egg yolk

5 eggs

2 cups whipping cream

¼ tsp freshly grated nutmeg

---

Heat the oven to 400°F.

Warm a large sauté pan over medium heat and melt the butter. Add the leeks and sauté until they are slightly browned and softened, about 12 minutes. Add a tablespoon or two of water if the pan gets too dry.

Add the wine to the pan and cook until the liquid is mostly absorbed, 5 minutes. Remove from heat, stir in the thyme, and season with salt and pepper. Set aside to cool.

On a lightly floured surface, roll out the pastry dough into a large circle, about ⅛-inch thick and large enough to line your pie plate. Transfer the dough into a 9- or 10-inch pie plate. Press the dough into the plate, and crimp the edges with your fingers to create an edge. Form the edge about ¼ inch higher than the finished product, as the dough will shrink slightly as it bakes.

Cut a circle of parchment paper with the same diameter as your pie plate and press it onto the dough. Pour baking beads or dry beans on top. Bake for 20 minutes. Take out of the oven, remove the beads and parchment, and turn down the oven to 350°F.

Line a rimmed sheet pan with parchment paper and place the pie plate on top.

Spread the Dijon over the bottom of the crust. Layer with the leek mixture, then dot the goat cheese over top. In a small cup, whisk together the egg yolk and 1 tsp water. Brush the edge of the crust with the egg yolk mixture.

In a medium-sized bowl, lightly whisk the eggs. Add the cream and the nutmeg and season with sea salt and pepper. Pour over the leeks and goat cheese.

Place the sheet pan with the pie plate on top in the oven and bake until crust is browned and the middle is only slightly jiggly, 30–40 minutes.

Let rest for 15 minutes before slicing and serving.

# POTATO AND MUSHROOM GALETTE

## SERVES 6–8

Mushroom foraging is very much a covert activity in our village of Villers-la-Faye, like it is in all the small villages of the Hautes-Côtes. Mushroom spots in the surrounding forests are absolutely top secret, and their locations are passed down for generations in a cloak and dagger fashion. If a local passes on a mushroom location to you, consider yourself privileged indeed. When leaving his house to go foraging, our next-door neighbor sneaks away with two wicker baskets and zig-zags his route to ensure no one is following him.

All pharmacists in France are trained in mushroom identification. If you have any doubts about your haul, take them to a pharmacist to have them checked over. I'm not hugely adventurous as far as mushrooms are concerned, so if you're like me, rest assured that even your store-bought champignons de Paris would be delicious in this comforting galette.

---

Place a large pot filled with water over high heat and bring to a boil. Add the salt. Cut the potatoes in half or in thirds (depending on size), add to the boiling water, and boil until fork-tender, 15–18 minutes. Drain and set aside to cool.

While the potatoes are boiling, warm a large frying pan over medium heat and melt the butter. Add the leeks and cook, stirring, until softened, about 15 minutes. Add the garlic and then the mushrooms and continue cooking, stirring often, until the mushrooms have released their liquid, about 10 minutes. Season with sea salt and pepper. Add the wine and cook until the liquid has mostly evaporated, about 10 minutes. Remove from the heat.

In a measuring cup, combine the cream, Dijon, and thyme. Season with salt and pepper and add to the mushroom mixture.

Slice the potatoes into ⅓-inch slices and fold them carefully into the mushrooms. If they break a bit, that's okay. Fold in the spinach. Taste and adjust seasoning.

Line a large rimmed sheet pan with parchment paper.

On a lightly floured surface, roll the dough into a circle about ⅛-inch thick and 15 inches in diameter. Transfer carefully onto the prepared sheet pan. Pile the potato mushroom mixture in the center, leaving a 2- or 3-inch border of pastry all round, and fold the pastry up and over the edge of the filling, overlapping as you go (you may need to trim a bit). Leave the pie open-faced. The crust should only overlap the filling by a few inches or so. Brush the pastry with the egg yolk and let sit in the fridge, covered, for about 30 minutes.

Heat the oven to 400°F.

Bake the galette until the pastry is brown and the filling is hot throughout, 25–35 minutes.

2 tsp kosher salt

2 lb Yukon gold or white potatoes, scrubbed

2 Tbsp unsalted butter

2 medium leeks, white and light-green parts sliced and washed

2 cloves garlic, minced

1 lb mixed mushrooms, sliced (cremini, oyster, shiitake, or any combo of your favorites)

½ cup dry white wine

¾ cup whipping cream

1 Tbsp Dijon mustard

1 Tbsp thyme leaves

3 packed cups spinach leaves, roughly chopped

1 recipe Basic Pastry (savory) (page 38)

1 egg yolk, whisked

# ROASTED MEUILLEY CHERRY TOMATOES AND CHICKEN

### SERVES 4–6

When we're at our house in Burgundy in the summer, we buy many of our veggies from a local winemaker's house in the nearby village of Meuilley. He makes wonderful wine, and he and his wife also have an impressive garden they operate as a side business during the summer months.

Locally in the Hautes-Côtes they are known for their cherry tomatoes. Mention the cherry tomatoes from Meuilley to anyone around Villers and they'll know exactly what you're talking about. Locals stream in and out of the wine domaine all day to buy bowls full of these shiny, bright red explosions of deliciousness. They are sweet and juicy and taste like the summer sun caught in a gorgeous little package.

Last summer I wanted to make some chicken for lunch, and I had a massive bowl of fresh Meuilley tomatoes on hand. Why not combine them into a simple dish that would highlight the incredible flavors of both, I thought? The result is this perfect dish. It's like summer on a plate.

2 Tbsp olive oil, divided

2½ lb chicken thighs, bone in, skin on (about 8 large)

2 cups cherry tomatoes, halved

8 cloves garlic, peeled and chopped

¼ cup balsamic vinegar

4–6 sprigs fresh rosemary

---

Heat the oven to 400° F.

Place a large ovenproof skillet over medium heat and add 1 Tbsp of the oil.

Season the chicken well with sea salt and pepper, place skin-side down in the skillet, and leave undisturbed until the skin is browned and crisp, 8–10 minutes.

In the meantime, combine the remaining 1 Tbsp oil, the tomatoes, garlic, and balsamic in a medium bowl. Season with salt and pepper and toss to combine.

Flip the chicken so it is skin-side up in the skillet. Pour the tomato mixture evenly over top. Lay the rosemary on top.

Transfer to the oven and bake until the chicken is cooked through, the tomatoes are cooked and juicy, and the garlic is softened, 35–45 minutes.

# SALMON PAPILLOTE
## with Franck's Asparagus

The idea of gathering together meat or fish, some herbs and spices, and some vegetables, tucking them all up in a neat little package of parchment paper, and baking the package is a stroke of genius. This technique helps flavors combine beautifully and also offers plenty of scope for innovation and creative flourish.

The asparagus in this recipe uses Franck's special technique of charring the asparagus stalks at a high heat in a cast iron pan. We all love this dish at home, as the charring and blistering somehow seals in the delicate asparagus flavor while leaving the asparagus stalk lovely and tender. It the perfect accompaniment to the delectable package of salmon—and countless other things as well.

---

Stir together the yogurt and lime juice, and then mix in the dill, cilantro, and red pepper flakes (if using). Season with sea salt and pepper. Cover and place in the fridge for at least 1 hour and up to overnight to allow the flavors to meld.

Bring a large pot of water to a boil. Add the whole potatoes and boil until fork-tender, 15–20 minutes. Add the asparagus and boil for another 3 minutes. Drain and rinse the potatoes and asparagus well with cold, running water.

While the vegetables are boiling, stir together the olive oil and lemon juice. Stir in the garlic and smoked paprika, add a pinch of sea salt, and set aside.

Heat the oven to 400°F.

Set out four large pieces of parchment paper (each about 15 x 20 inches) with the long side facing you. Slice the potatoes into about ⅛-inch-thick rounds. Place the potato slices in the center of each piece of parchment in two or three vertical rows, slightly overlapping. Season generously with salt and pepper. Drizzle one quarter of the oil mixture over the potatoes and place a salmon fillet vertically on top. Sprinkle with a pinch of sea salt and pepper. Top with lemon and red onion slices.

To make the *papillote*, fold both short sides of each piece of parchment over top of the salmon. You want each end covered by about 1 inch. Now bring the long sides up to meet in the middle above the salmon and fold them over on themselves four or five times to create a tight fold. Tuck everything in underneath the entire pack to create a neat parcel. Place the packs on a rimmed sheet pan and bake until the potatoes are fully cooked and the salmon is medium-rare (about 120°F), 15–18 minutes. Once you've checked the temperature, fold the fish back up in the parchment to rest for 5 minutes. (Another way you can tell if the salmon is cooked is to flake it with a fork. If it comes apart easily, but is still moist and glistening, it is ready.)

While the fish is cooking, warm a large cast iron pan over high heat and then add the vegetable oil. Once the oil is hot, add the asparagus and cook, rolling around, until all the edges are slightly blistered and browned, 5–7 minutes. Season with salt and pepper. CONTINUED ON PAGE 115.

1 cup full-fat plain yogurt

2 Tbsp lime juice (1–2 limes)

1 packed Tbsp minced dill

1 packed Tbsp minced cilantro

Pinch red pepper flakes (optional)

4 medium-sized white or yellow potatoes

1 lb asparagus, trimmed

¼ cup olive oil

2 tsp lemon juice

1 clove garlic, minced

1 tsp smoked paprika

4 (each 6 oz) salmon fillets, skinless, bones removed

1 lemon, thinly sliced

½ red onion, thinly sliced

1 Tbsp vegetable oil (any oil with a high smoking point)

Plate the potatoes and salmon with their onion and lemon slices, making sure you pour any residual smoked paprika oil over top. Top with the asparagus and drizzle with about 2 Tbsp of the yogurt sauce. Serve with the remaining yogurt sauce in a bowl on the side.

*Potatoes and salmon have very different cooking times. The trick is to ensure they spend enough time in the oven to cook them both sufficiently without overcooking the fish. Boil the potatoes until they feel a bit soft and the knife goes through with only a very slight resistance. Slice them as thinly as you can.—RW*

# BEEF BOURGUIGNON
## with Homemade Egg Noodles

When I think of the ultimate Burgundian dish, boeuf bourguignon and coq au vin are pretty much head to head, but if I *had* to choose, I think boeuf bourguignon would win by a smidgen. All the cooks in Franck's family (and there are many of them—just a wee bit intimidating for this here foreign family member) can whip up a medal-worthy boeuf bourguignon.

The best I ever tasted was at our friend Martial's house. One dark winter night at around seven o'clock Martial called us. "Do you want to come down to Ladoix and have dinner with us? I . . . uh . . . made a little error with my boeuf bourguignon." Intrigued, we hopped in the car and zoomed down the hill to his house. Most of Martial's wine was chalk-marked unlabeled bottles from winemaker friends and family. By mistake, he had poured a 1991 Vougeot Premier Cru, Les Petits Vougeots, into his boeuf bourguignon instead of a Hautes-Côtes Villages. That was the best darn boeuf bourguignon I have ever tasted by a *mile*. When people tell you any old wine can be used for boeuf bourguignon, don't believe it for a second. The better the wine, the better the dish.

Like so many stewed meat dishes, boeuf bourguignon is even better the next day. This was the main dish at our wedding reception in a wine cellar in Nuits-Saint-Georges, in keeping with Burgundy tradition.

---

Heat the oven to 325°F.

Place a large Dutch oven over medium heat and fry the bacon until crisp and brown, about 5 minutes. Using a slotted spoon, transfer the bacon to a large bowl, leaving the fat in the pot.

Dry the beef well between paper towels and season it generously on all sides with salt and pepper.

Increase the heat to medium-high and brown the beef in the bacon fat on all sides, 3–4 minutes per side. You will need to do this in batches. Add the browned beef to the bowl with the bacon.

Add the oil to the pot. Cook the onions until softened, about 5 minutes, scraping up any brown bits from the bottom of the pot. Add the garlic and carrots and cook for another minute.

Return the beef and bacon to the pot. Sprinkle in the flour and stir well to coat, cooking for another 2 minutes. Pour in the wine and stir in the tomato paste to combine thoroughly. Add just enough of the stock so that it just barely covers the beef. Throw in the bay leaves and thyme. Cook, uncovered, on the stovetop for 10 minutes, stirring to cook the flour and combine the flavors. Remove from the heat.

Place a large piece of parchment paper over the beef, pressing down so it is tight against the beef and comes up the insides of the pot. This seals in the steam and the juices and allows the beef to become beautifully tender and juicy. Cover

6 slices thick-cut bacon, cut into ⅓-inch pieces

3 lb stewing beef

2 Tbsp vegetable oil

1 large onion, thinly sliced

6 garlic cloves, thinly sliced, lengthwise

1 large carrot, peeled and sliced into coins

2 Tbsp all-purpose flour

2 cups deep, dark red wine (Pinot noir if possible! And preferably Burgundy pinot.)

2 Tbsp tomato paste

2–3 cups Beef Stock (page 25 or store-bought)

3 bay leaves

5 sprigs fresh thyme

18–24 pearl onions

4 Tbsp butter

1 lb button mushrooms, stems trimmed (or if you can't find button, regular-sized mushrooms, cut in half)

¼ cup parsley

1 recipe Homemade Egg Noodles (page 118)

the pot with its lid and place it in the oven. Let it cook until the beef is fall-apart tender, about 3 hours.

At the 2½-hour point, prepare the pearl onions and mushrooms.

Fill a large pot with water and bring to a boil over high heat. Throw in the pearl onions and boil for 1 minute. Rinse with cold water and strain. This will make them much easier to peel. Peel them and leave them whole.

Place a large sauté pan over medium heat and melt the butter. Add the pearl onions and mushrooms and cook until tender, stirring to keep everything coated with butter, 5–7 minutes.

Remove the beef from the oven, stir the onions and mushrooms into the cooked stew, and sprinkle with parsley. Serve over homemade egg noodles.

# Homemade Egg Noodles

SERVES 4-6

There is a marked difference between homemade noodles and dry noodles, and once you get the hang of them, it is not a terrible chore to make your own. If you find a good-quality egg noodle that you can purchase, however, we promise you will still love this dish!

This recipe doubles easily, but I recommend separating and kneading the dough in two batches, as it will be much easier to handle.—RW

2 cups all-purpose flour, plus more for dusting

2 whole large eggs

4 large egg yolks

1 tsp kosher salt, plus more for salting water

On a large, clean work surface, pour the flour into a pile, making a well in the center, about 4 inches wide. Make sure there are walls of flour around the well.

Drop the eggs and yolks into the well and whisk gently with a fork. Don't worry if some of the flour sneaks in at this point. Add the salt.

Using a fork, drag the flour gently into the eggs. Continue to do this all around the well until all the flour is incorporated into the eggs and a shaggy, rough dough comes together.

Using your hands (and a bench scraper if necessary), gather all the mixture together and start to knead. This will take some time, but just when you think all hope is lost, it will come together.

Mix and knead and gather for a good 10–15 minutes until a smooth and very firm dough is formed. If the dough is too wet, add flour 1 tsp at a time; if the dough is too dry, add water with a spray bottle to distribute it evenly. It is difficult to over-knead pasta dough, so don't be afraid to work hard at this.

Once the ball of dough has come together and is nice and smooth, wrap it in plastic wrap and leave on the counter for at least 30 minutes. If you are making the noodles ahead of time, feel free to pop it in the fridge overnight, but ensure you take it out at least 30 minutes before you need to roll it out.

A pasta roller is definitely the best bet for rolling out this dough. They are not expensive and are a good little investment if you feel you might do this more than once. If you cannot get your hands on one, you can use a straight-edged rolling pin and place a thin metal ruler on each side of the dough as you roll it thinner to obtain consistency in the thickness of the dough. Either way, you want to get a nice thin dough for these noodles.

Line a large sheet pan with parchment paper and dust it lightly with flour.

Remove the plastic wrap from the dough and, using a bench scraper, cut the dough into four pieces. Work with one piece at a time, and cover the rest of the dough with plastic wrap. Following the manufacturer's instructions for the pasta roller or by rolling manually, roll the dough to about the thickness of a metal ruler (typically the thinnest or second-thinnest setting on the pasta roller). Start with the biggest setting on the machine, then fold the pasta sheet in half and re-run it through the machine, changing the dial to a thinner setting each time you pass the dough through. Place the finished sheets of pasta on the prepared sheet pan and sprinkle lightly with flour to prevent sticking. Using a knife or pasta roller attachment, cut into strips of your desired width and toss with a bit of flour. Repeat with the remaining pasta dough.

Bring a large pot full of well-salted water to a boil over high heat. Add the desired amount of pasta and cook for about 1 minute, taste, and either cook for another 30–60 seconds if needed or drain. Serve with beef bourguignon (page 117) or your favorite pasta sauce.

# COQ AU VIN WITH WHITE WINE

## SERVES 4–6

A close second to boeuf bourguignon (page 117), coq au vin is also one of Burgundy's regional specialties. Mémé, Franck's grandmother, made the ultimate coq au vin in the traditional way. She would go to the *boucherie* and buy a rooster (sometimes live, sometimes not) and a nice fresh batch of chicken blood to cook up her coq au vin.

When I first learned, after a year or two of reveling in her delicious coq au vin, that Mémé added fresh blood I was put off . . . for a second or two. Then I shrugged and kept eating. It was that delicious.

For years at La Maison des Chaumes, our house in Villers-la-Faye, we were woken up by the crowing of roosters belonging to our neighbor across the street, an ancient Italian woman called Inès who had the most stunning espaliered fruit trees in her garden. Every once in a while, her roosters would fall silent, and Franck and I would joke that Inès had just made a fresh batch of coq au vin.

Rebecca has done a brilliant job of adapting the traditional recipe, as neither fresh chicken blood nor roosters are easy to come by outside of France. She has used more accessible ingredients to create a dish that is as satisfying and delicious as the original.

---

Heat the oven to 350°F.

Heat the oil over medium heat in a large ovenproof sauté pan (at least 5-quart capacity). Add the bacon, and cook until crispy, 8–10 minutes. Using a slotted spoon, transfer it to a bowl and set aside.

Pat the chicken pieces dry with paper towel and season generously on all sides with sea salt and pepper. Add the chicken to the bacon fat in two batches, skin-side down. (Add a tablespoon or two of vegetable oil if the pan is too dry.) Sear for about 5 minutes on each side, until the skin is rendered, crispy, and browned. Transfer to a large plate and set aside.

Add the diced onion and carrots to the pan, and cook over medium heat for 7 minutes, stirring occasionally, until onions are translucent and lightly browned. Add the garlic, and cook until fragrant, about 1 minute.

Pour in the stock, wine, and brandy, stirring to combine. Add half the bacon, the chicken and any juices left on the plate, and 5 sprigs of the thyme. Check that the chicken is skin-side up and not immersed fully in the liquid to keep the skin from going soggy.

Place a large piece of parchment paper over the chicken, pressing down so it is tight against the top of the ingredients and comes down the insides of the pot. This seals in the steam and the juices and allows the chicken to become beautifully tender and juicy. Cover the pot with its lid, or tightly with aluminum foil, and place in the oven. CONTINUED ON PAGE 123.

2 Tbsp olive oil

12 strips bacon, cut into ½-inch slices

8 chicken pieces (4 drumsticks and 4 thighs), skin on, bone in

1 large onion, diced

2 medium-sized carrots, sliced

4 cloves garlic, minced

1½ cups Chicken Stock (page 26 or store-bought)

1½ cups dry white wine

¼ cup brandy

8 sprigs thyme, divided

10 oz pearl onions

2 Tbsp butter

1 lb small button or cremini mushrooms, thickly sliced

½ cup Crème Fraîche (page 30 or store-bought)

1 tsp Dijon mustard

¼ cup tarragon leaves to garnish

Bake until the chicken is cooked through, 35–40 minutes.

While the chicken is in the oven, bring a small pot of water to a boil and add the pearl onions. Boil for 1 minute, then drain. Peel the pearl onions.

Melt the butter in a sauté pan over medium heat. Cook the mushrooms and pearl onions until softened and browned, 8–10 minutes. Add the leaves from the 2 remaining thyme sprigs.

Season with salt and pepper. Set aside.

Remove the pot from the oven and transfer the chicken to a plate. Strain the cooking liquid through a fine-mesh sieve, pushing down on the contents to extract as much broth as possible. Discard the solids and return the liquid to the pot. Whisk in the crème fraîche and Dijon. Bring to a simmer and cook until reduced and slightly thickened, about 10 minutes.

Taste and season with salt and pepper. Add the chicken, bacon, mushrooms, and pearl onions to the pot.

Simmer for 5 minutes to heat the chicken through, garnish with the tarragon, and serve.

# SALADE NIÇOISE

## SERVES 4

When it is 100°F outside in the summer in France, sometimes salad-as-a-meal sounds just right. Even though salade niçoise was developed in the South of France, when the thermometer rises so does the urgent need to make a salade niçoise as a one-dish meal.

I make this at least a few times every summer for a family lunch, and even though the ingredients are simple, combined they make a truly delicious (not to mention well-balanced) meal. Also, if you are in an artistic mood, you can get very imaginative with the placement of the ingredients on the platter—my girls love helping me do this—and create a veritable work of art. Beautiful and delicious.

4 eggs

1 lb baby potatoes, scrubbed and halved

½ lb fresh green beans, trimmed

1 lb fresh ahi or albacore tuna fillet

1 Tbsp vegetable oil

8 cups fresh mixed greens of your choice

1 recipe Mme Beaupré's Homemade Vinaigrette (page 21)

1 cup cherry tomatoes, halved

1 small English cucumber, sliced

½ cup niçoise olives

Set a steamer basket in a medium pot with about 1 inch of water over high heat. Place the eggs in the basket and cover. Bring to a boil, turn down the heat to medium, and let steam for 7 minutes. Rinse the eggs under cold running water for 1 minute and set aside.

Place a large pot filled with water over high heat. Bring to a boil and add the potatoes. Boil for 10 minutes, then add the beans. Boil for another 5 minutes or until the potatoes are fork-tender and the beans are softened but still snappy. Strain and rinse under cold, running water for 30 seconds. Drain well and set aside.

Season the tuna on all sides with sea salt and pepper.

Heat a large cast iron pan over medium heat. Add the oil. Once the oil is shimmering, place the tuna gently in it and cook for 30 seconds. Flip and cook for another 30 seconds. Remove from the heat and transfer to a cutting board. Tent loosely with aluminum foil.

Place the greens in a large salad bowl. Toss with the desired amount of vinaigrette.

Slice the tuna on the diagonal and against the grain into ¼-inch slices. Place on top of the greens. Add the potatoes and beans, tomatoes, cucumber, and olives. Peel the eggs and carefully cut them in half lengthwise. Add to the salad, drizzle with more vinaigrette, and season with salt and pepper. Serve immediately.

# MUSSELS WITH LEMON AND SHALLOTS

## SERVES 4–6

Whenever we go to Paris, we stay at our friend Jacinthe's apartment in Montparnasse, which means whenever we go to Paris, we go out for moules-frites.

Let me explain. Paris has four train stations, and each of them services a different direction in France (north, south, east, or west). "Our" Paris train station, for example, is the Gare de Lyon, which services the south. The Gare Montparnasse services northwestern France, so a high population of Northerners live in that *quartier*. What is a typical northern French dish? Why, mussels and fries, *bien sûr*. There is therefore a proliferation of Paris's best moules-frites restaurants around Jacinthe's apartment, and we hit one up every time we stay with her. When I think of moules-frites, I think of wonderful Parisian evenings spent with my dear friend who has been with me through thick and thin.

In a large pot with a tight-fitting lid, melt the butter over medium heat. Add the shallots and cook until softened, 5–7 minutes. Add the garlic and cook for another 2 minutes, stirring frequently.

Add the wine and increase the heat to high. Once the wine is boiling, gently add the mussels, being careful not to break any. Place the lid on the pot and turn down the heat to medium.

Cook the mussels until they are all open, 4–6 minutes. Using a slotted spoon, remove them from the pot and place them in a large bowl. Discard any that did not open.

Whisk the lemon zest and juice into the cooking liquid in the pot, followed by the cream and Dijon. Add the tomatoes, parsley, and thyme and season to taste with sea salt and pepper.

Return the mussels to the pot for 30 seconds, just to heat, and then gently pour them into a large bowl to serve with lemon wedges, aioli, and plenty of bread or frites.

3 Tbsp butter

4 large shallots, thinly sliced

3 cloves garlic, thinly sliced

1 cup dry white wine

4 lb fresh mussels

Grated zest of 1 large lemon

2 Tbsp fresh lemon juice

¼ cup whipping cream

1 Tbsp Dijon mustard

1 large tomato, pulp and seeds removed, then diced

¼ cup chopped parsley

1 Tbsp thyme leaves

Lemon wedges to serve

Lemon Aioli (page 29) to serve

Baguette or French Bread (page 159) or frites to serve

*Depending on where you purchase your fresh mussels, they may come with beards, a small bunch of elastic-like threads that help hold a mussel to a solid surface, such as a rock. The beard can't harm you, but it doesn't really have a desirable mouthfeel. It is found peeking out of the shell and can easily be torn out using your fingers or a pair of needle-nose pliers. Before cooking mussels, be aware that you only want live ones, which are identified by being fully closed. If you spot any mussels that are slightly agape, give them a gentle tap on the counter. If they close on their own, they are ready to cook. If they don't, discard them. Furthermore, if any mussels do not open once cooked, they are to be discarded as well.—RW*

# OEUFS EN MEURETTE
## *with White Wine*

**SERVES 6**

Oeufs en meurette, basically poached eggs in wine sauce, is another classic Burgundy dish and was traditionally made with leftover sauce from the previous day's coq au vin. It's a peasant dish, as are so many of the best dishes. It is usually made with red wine, but I have tasted the white wine variation a few times and it is truly something special.

There is a wonderful restaurant in Volnay, where my friend Marc-Olivier's family wine domaine is located. It has been around for decades and specializes in traditional Burgundian fare served under the stone arches of a wine cellar. They don't always have a white wine oeufs en meurette on the menu, but this was the first place I ever tasted this variation, and it was truly a spectacular Burgundian experience I will never forget.

---

Place the shallots, garlic, and onions in a food processor and pulse until finely minced, but not mushy.

Place a large sauté pan over medium heat. Add 1 Tbsp of the oil and cook the lardons (or bacon pieces) until just starting to crisp. Add the mushrooms and continue to cook until they release their liquid, about 5 minutes. Using a slotted spoon, transfer the lardons and mushrooms to a bowl. Set aside.

Pour the remaining 1 Tbsp oil into the hot pan then add the onion mixture. Turn down the heat to medium-low and cook, stirring often to prevent the onions from getting too brown, until they have softened, about 5 minutes. Pour the wine into the mixture and stir to combine. Add the bouquet garni and quatre épices and let simmer until the wine has reduced by about half, 10–12 minutes. Remove from the heat.

Heat the oven to broil.

Place a saucepan over medium heat and melt 2 Tbsp of the butter. Whisk in the flour and continue whisking to allow the flour to cook, about 3 minutes. The mixture should be the consistency of thick paste. Pour in the stock, whisking constantly, bring to a slow boil, and stir gently with a wooden spoon until the stock has thickened, 3–5 minutes. Add the cream and stir to combine.

Remove the bouquet garni from the onion mixture and add the onion mixture to the thickened stock. Season to taste with sea salt and pepper. Remove from the heat and cover to keep warm.

Bring a large pot of water to a boil on high heat and then add the vinegar.

Place the baguette slices on a parchment-lined sheet pan and rub with the cut garlic clove. Spread with the remaining 3 Tbsp butter and broil until toasty and brown, 4–5 minutes.

Crack one egg into each of four ramekins or small, shallow bowls. Give the

2 shallots, roughly chopped

2 garlic cloves, roughly chopped

1 small onion, roughly chopped

2 Tbsp olive oil, divided

4 oz lardons or bacon, cut into ¼-inch pieces

2 cups sliced shiitake mushrooms

2 cups dry white wine

1 bouquet garni of 5 sprigs thyme, 1 sprig rosemary, and 2 bay leaves (page 19)

1 tsp Quatre Épices (page 19)

5 Tbsp butter, divided

2 Tbsp all-purpose flour

1 cup Chicken Stock or Vegetable Broth (page 26 or store-bought)

2 cups heavy cream

2 Tbsp white vinegar

Baguette, sliced into 12 (¾-inch) pieces

1 garlic clove, halved

6–12 large eggs (depending on how hungry your guests are!)

2 Tbsp minced parsley

water a good stir so you create a whirlpool effect and gently slide each egg into the center of the whirlpool. Simmer the eggs for 3 or 4 minutes (depending on how you like them), then use a slotted spoon to transfer them to a plate lined with a paper towel. Cover with foil to keep them warm while you poach the remaining eggs.

While the eggs are poaching, place two baguette slices on the bottom of each of six shallow bowls. Divide the mushrooms and lardons evenly between the bowls. Pour a bit of the sauce over the bread, top with one or two poached eggs, and divide the remaining sauce between the bowls. Season with salt and pepper and sprinkle with the parsley.

# SIMPLE-ISH CASSOULET

### SERVES 6–8

Cassoulet is creamy and rich and hearty and pretty much the ultimate comfort dish. It hails from farther south than Burgundy—from the Languedoc region, which specializes in poultry products—but it has been embraced by people from all over France.

On cold, rainy days we used to go to a restaurant in Paris that specialized in the cuisine of southwestern France. We liked to go for lunch and order the cassoulet. The waiter would place a cast iron Le Creuset casserole dish on the table between us, and we would serve ourselves platefuls of the fragrant concoction of creamy beans, sausage, and duck (although we use easier-to-find chicken in this recipe), using slices of baguette to soak up every last bit of sauce as the rain pelted down on the gray street outside. Needless to say, we dispensed with dinner!

Pour the beans into a large bowl or pot, cover with 16 cups of water, and add the salt. Stir to combine and leave overnight to soak. When morning comes (because cassoulet takes a while, so starting in the morning is smart), drain the beans and set aside.

Place a large Dutch oven over medium heat. Add the salt pork and fry it until the fat is rendered and the pieces are crispy on all sides, about 10 minutes. Using a slotted spoon, transfer to a large bowl.

Place the sausages in the pot and fry on all sides until browned, about 5 minutes. Add them to the bowl with the pork. Drain all but 1 Tbsp of fat from the pot and add the 1 Tbsp duck fat (if using). If you're not using duck fat, leave about 2 Tbsp of fat in the pot.

Season the chicken with pepper and add to the pot skin-side down (you will need to cook this in batches). Let sit undisturbed for about 8 minutes. Flip and cook for another 4 minutes. Transfer to the bowl with the sausage and repeat with the remaining chicken. Drain all but 1 Tbsp of fat from the pot.

Add the onions and celery to the pot and cook for 5 minutes, stirring frequently to avoid too much browning. Add the wine and scrape up any brown bits from the bottom of the pot.

Add the drained beans, garlic, cloves, bay leaves, and stock to the pot, bring to a simmer, cover, and cook until the beans are tender, about 45 minutes.

Heat the oven to 300°F.

Remove the cloves and bay leaves from the pot. Peel the garlic, mash it into a paste with a fork, and stir it into the beans. Add the salt pork and sausages, stirring to combine. Lay the chicken pieces on top of the beans, pushing some down to make room for them all.

Place in the oven, uncovered, and cook for 2 hours. Check occasionally that the beans are fully submerged. If they're not, pour a bit of water down the side of

1 lb dry cannellini beans

1½ Tbsp kosher salt

12 oz salt pork, cut into ¾-inch cubes

3 links Toulouse sausage (or any mild, garlic pork sausage), cut into 1-inch pieces

1 Tbsp duck fat (optional)

6 pieces chicken (3 legs and 3 thighs), skin on, bone in

1 large onion, julienned

2 stalks celery, finely diced

½ cup dry white wine

1 whole head garlic, most but not all of the papery skin peeled off

10 whole cloves, tucked into a square of cheesecloth and tied with kitchen twine

3 bay leaves

4 cups Chicken Stock (page 26 or store-bought)

¼ cup minced curly parsley

the pot, so as not to disturb the crust forming.

At the 2-hour point, pull the cassoulet from the oven and give it a little shake. Again, ensure the beans are fully submerged and, if not, add a bit of water. If the chicken skin is getting dry, baste it with some of the broth. Return to the oven for another 2½ hours, checking in every 30 minutes to add water and to shake the pot to distribute and cook the beans evenly.

At the 4½-hour point, check that the top is nice and brown. If not, return to the oven for another 30–60 minutes. Everything will simply continue to deepen in flavor and become more delicious. Expect a total of 4–5 hours of oven time.

When you do remove from the heat, sprinkle with parsley and serve immediately.

---

# Cassoulet

Simple-ish? Really? Okay, maybe that's a stretch. There's never anything really simple about making cassoulet, but this version cuts down on a few steps. And mostly, the time needed is time in the oven, so there is lots of space to do other things while it's bubbling away. While there are myriad tips from different chefs about how to perfect cassoulet, I have outlined a few basics below to ensure you have everything in your arsenal to make your best version of this classic dish.

ON DUCK VS. CHICKEN Making or sourcing duck confit, a traditional ingredient in this dish, isn't for everyone. Luckily, substituting easily obtained chicken and then cooking it in duck fat is a perfectly acceptable, if not traditional alternative. Duck fat has a distinct flavor, and so, if you can find it, I highly recommend using it. The bonus is that it keeps in the fridge for at least 3 months. If you're stuck on tradition, you can, of course, make your own duck confit, and you might even find prepared duck confit at your butcher. If you decide to go for it, simply replace the chicken with duck in the recipe.

ON SEASONING I can be rather liberal with the salt shaker, so you might be surprised to find that there is no extra salt added during cooking. Salting the beans overnight—a rather controversial step, as many claim salting can make the beans tough—ensures the beans are seasoned throughout and flavors the entire dish. Due to the long, slow cooking time, these beans will definitely end up nice and tender. Furthermore, salt pork is very effective at bringing the seasoning right up to par. If possible, have a word with your butcher when you're buying it, as some salt pork is very salty and needs a good overnight soak to mellow some of that salty intensity. If you can't find salt pork, you can replace it with a nice garlicy pork coil sausage, though we are straying even further from tradition! (I'm okay with that.) Alternatively, you can make your own salt pork by heavily salting a portion of pork belly and leaving it in the fridge for 3 days. Check online for more detailed directions if you choose to go this route. Last resort? Use thick-cut bacon and adjust the seasonings accordingly.

**ON CRUST AND CHICKEN STOCK** As one of the main objectives of a good cassoulet is a deep, rich crust on top, some people add fine breadcrumbs at the tail end of baking, and you are welcome to do that, too. However, your stock will play a big part in the development of that crust on top. If your chicken stock is homemade with bones and has been slowly simmered, chances are it will be quite gelatinous when refrigerated. That natural gelatin will aid in creating a lovely crust on top of the cassoulet. I will always recommend homemade chicken stock, as in my opinion it is undeniably superior, but I do get that sometimes that is just not an option. If you are using store-bought chicken stock, you can leave it as is, or you can add 2½ Tbsp unflavored gelatin to it to help the crust form.

**ON TIME** Traditional cassoulet is in the oven for many hours, often up to 6 or 7! We've left our version at 4½ hours, give or take, and it turns out fantastic. If you have the time, and are so inclined, continue to cook to deepen and enrich the flavors, but know that the beans will continue to cook, which means they will become quite a bit softer. If you like that, keep adding water if needed to keep the beans submerged and baste the chicken if the skin is getting too dry.

**THE BOTTOM LINE** Cassoulet is a peasant dish. A soupy stew meant to use up scraps of meat and broth and beans, all thrown into a pot, and simmered for a long time. Having said that, use quality ingredients, cook low and slow, and even if you don't obtain the perfect, somewhat elusive crust, I promise it will be a delicious and satisfying meal.—RW

# RUSTIC LENTIL AND POTATO STEW

SERVES 6–8

I'm a wee bit obsessed with lentils. The best ones come from the Puy region in central France, and I always try to use those if I can. They hold their shape and firmness and don't become brown mush. In France I frequently enjoy cold lentil salad as well as warm lentils. Rebecca has created this comforting lentil and potato stew for when you need something warm and nutritious in your belly.

If you keep your pantry stocked with Puy lentils, you can throw this dish together with minimal planning and sit down just over half an hour later to eat. It's lovely served with toasted baguette and a crisp green salad.

Place the oil in a large pot over medium-high heat. Once shimmering, add the celery and leeks and cook until softened, 5–7 minutes. Add the garlic, bay leaves, and chili flakes and cook for another minute.

Stir in the lentils. Add the stock, bring to a boil, then simmer, uncovered, over medium-low heat for 10 minutes.

Add the potatoes. Simmer for another 20–30 minutes, or until the lentils and potatoes are tender and the stew is thick. Turn down the heat to low. Stir in the chard, rosemary, lemon zest, and lemon juice. Season well with kosher salt and pepper. Top with the cilantro and crème fraîche (if using).

3 Tbsp olive oil

2 celery stalks, diced

2 medium leeks, chopped, white and light-green parts only

2 cloves garlic, minced

2 bay leaves

½ tsp chili flakes

1 cup Puy lentils or French green lentils, rinsed (see note)

6 cups Chicken Stock or Vegetable Broth (page 26 or store-bought)

1½ lb white or yellow baby potatoes, chopped into bite-sized pieces

1 bunch chard, roughly chopped (kale or spinach work here, too)

1 Tbsp rosemary, minced

2 tsp grated lemon zest

2 Tbsp fresh lemon juice

Fresh cilantro and Crème Fraîche (page 30) for serving (optional)

*A word about lentils. Puy lentils and French green lentils are essentially the same, but Puy lentils are grown in the Puy region of central France, while French green lentils are not. They are a small, mottled green/gray lentil that cooks in 20–30 minutes. Other lentils will work in this recipe, though I would avoid red or yellow lentils, as they cook very quickly and tend to get mushy and lose their shape. Brown lentils, on the other hand, are a good replacement. In any case, purchase only fresh lentils if you can, as the older they are the tougher they are. Always rinse them and check for small stones before cooking them. —RW*

# BOUILLABAISSE

## SERVES 6–8

This is another recipe that comes from the South of France but has become a beloved dish all over the country. Marseille fishers developed bouillabaisse as a way to use up the bony rockfish that tended to be too lowly and unattractive to sell from the docks.

Fittingly, the first time I tried bouillabaisse was at a restaurant in the fishing port of Marseille, watching the fishers come into port with their wares. I've never been a massive lover of fish and seafood (which is pretty ungrateful for a person brought up on their dad's freshly caught Pacific salmon) but bouillabaisse, in that moment, was the perfect thing to be eating.

Besides the fish, vegetables such as leeks, onions, tomatoes, celery, and potatoes are simmered with the broth. The broth is traditionally served with a rouille, a mayonnaise made of olive oil, garlic, saffron, and cayenne pepper spread on grilled slices of bread. Rebecca has created her own spin on bouillabaisse, which makes it perfect for a cook who is not within the radius of the Marseille docks.

---

Place the bell peppers, garlic, and almonds in a food processor and blend until almost smooth. Add the aioli (or mayonnaise) and lemon juice and blend to combine. (If using homemade lemon aioli, skip the lemon juice here.) Scoop into a small bowl, cover, and place in the fridge.

In a small bowl, soak the saffron in the orange juice. Set aside.

Peel the prawns, reserving the shells. Store the prawn meat in the fridge until you're ready to cook.

Place the oil in a large, heavy-bottomed pot over medium heat. Sauté the onion and chopped fennel in the oil until softened, but not browned, 5–7 minutes. Add the garlic and cook for another minute. Add the reserved prawn shells and cook for another 2 minutes. If you have access to fish heads and frames and other shells (ask your fishmonger, as they often sell these things very cheaply), add these now. Be sure that the fish heads and frames, etc., are very fresh, otherwise your stock will be much too fishy and essentially ruined. The broth is great without them, but it will have a stronger seafood flavor if you do use them. Pour in the stock and wine and then add the saffron (if using) and orange juice, peppercorns, bay leaves, and thyme. Simmer gently to meld all the flavors, about 30 minutes. Strain through a fine-mesh sieve and discard the solids.

Return the broth to the pot over medium heat and add the tomatoes, butter, and cayenne. Season to taste with salt and pepper, remembering that the seafood will add saltiness as well. Bring the broth to a simmer.

Cut the white fish into 2-inch pieces and throw into the pot. Stir so the fish is under the broth. Cook for 1 minute. CONTINUED ON PAGE 140.

½ cup roasted red bell peppers

1 small garlic clove, chopped

3 Tbsp chopped toasted almonds

¼ cup Lemon Aioli (page 29) or good-quality mayonnaise

2 tsp lemon juice

½ tsp saffron threads (optional)

¼ cup freshly squeezed orange juice

1 lb prawns, shell on, heads off

2 Tbsp olive oil

1 small onion, roughly chopped

2 large fennel bulbs, roughly chopped, fronds reserved

6 large garlic cloves, peeled and smashed

White fish heads, gills removed, fish frames, crab or lobster shells from your fishmonger (optional)

8 cups Vegetable Broth (page 26 or store-bought)

1 cup dry white wine

1 tsp whole peppercorns

2 bay leaves

5 sprigs thyme

Increase the heat to medium-high and bring the broth to a gentle boil. Add the mussels and clams and cover the pot. Cook for 3 minutes. Add the prawn meat, cover again, and cook for another 2 minutes. Check that all of the mussels and clams have opened. Discard any that haven't.

Ladle the seafood into bowls and add some broth over top. Garnish with the reserved fennel fronds and whole prawns (if using). Serve immediately with the toasted baguette and red pepper sauce.

1 cup fresh or drained, canned diced tomatoes

1 Tbsp unsalted butter

Pinch cayenne pepper

1 lb white fish (cod, halibut, monkfish, rockfish, or something similar)

1 lb mussels, cleaned

1 lb clams, cleaned

Cooked whole prawns (with heads) for garnish (optional)

1 baguette, cut diagonally and toasted

# PRUNE-STUFFED PORK WITH PROSCIUTTO

SERVES 6–8

I learned how to make rôti de porc with prunes when we were renovating our very first vacation rental in France, which I wrote all about in *My Grape Escape*. I was recovering from a post-Oxford law school nervous breakdown and very much needed Burgundy to teach me how to enjoy life again.

One of Franck's friends, Alain, helped us install our new windows. Like many French tradespeople, Alain is an expert on many things besides his line of work—such as the poems of Victor Hugo, 17th-century antiques, and wine, of course. He is also an expert chef and cooked us this delectable combination of ingredients for lunch one day during the window installation.

Rebecca has taken Alain's recipe one step further by stuffing the pork roast with the prune mixture and adding the deliciousness of prosciutto. I think Alain would approve.

---

Place the prunes in a large measuring cup and pour the Calvados over top. Pour in enough boiling water to just cover the prunes. Stir in the zest. Let sit, covered, for at least 30 minutes and up to overnight in the fridge.

Heat the oven to 430°F.

In a small bowl, mix together the Dijon, olive oil, garlic, and sage. Set aside.

Season the pork loin generously on all sides with sea salt and pepper. Drain the prunes, reserving the liquid, and line them up in the center of the inside of the pork. Roll the loin up and secure it with butcher's twine.

Place a large Dutch oven on the stovetop over medium-high heat. Add the vegetable oil. Once it's hot, sear the rolled pork on all sides, until the fat is rendered, browned, and crispy, 7–10 minutes in total. Transfer the pork to a plate.

Add the potatoes and onions to the Dutch oven and turn down the heat to medium. Cook until the potatoes are slightly browned, about 10 minutes. Season with a bit of salt and pepper. Remove from the heat.

Slather the pork on all sides with the Dijon mixture. Wrap the prosciutto slices tightly around the pork. They may not make it all the way around, and that's okay.

Arrange the potatoes and onions evenly on the bottom of the Dutch oven and pour ½ cup of water over top. Place the pork on top of the potatoes, tucking the loose ends of the prosciutto in underneath the pork.

Roast in the oven, uncovered, until the internal temperature reaches 145°F, 35–45 minutes. Remove the pork from the Dutch oven, place it on a large platter.

Using a slotted spoon, remove the potatoes and onions and place them on the platter around the pork. Tent the whole platter loosely with foil and let rest

1 cup pitted prunes

¼ cup Calvados

2 tsp grated orange zest

3 Tbsp Dijon mustard

2 tsp olive oil

2 garlic cloves, minced

2 Tbsp minced sage

3½ lb boneless, skinless pork loin, butterflied (Have your butcher do this for you! Also, have them slice off about half of the fat cap, so only about ¼ inch of cap is left on the loin.)

2 Tbsp vegetable oil

2 lb yellow or white potatoes, cut into wedges

1 small onion, julienned

3½ oz sliced prosciutto (4–5 large slices)

¾ cup Chicken Stock (page 26 or store-bought)

3 Tbsp butter

1 Tbsp lemon juice

for about 10 minutes. The pork will continue to cook slightly and the potatoes will keep warm.

Meanwhile, strain the liquid contents of the Dutch oven into a small saucepan. This may be mere scrapings, but that's okay. We're after the flavor here. Strain the prune poaching liquid into the saucepan as well, followed by the stock. Bring to a soft boil over medium-high heat and cook until the liquid has reduced by about one third, about 10 minutes. Remove from the heat and stir in the butter and lemon juice. Season well with salt and pepper.

Slice the pork and serve with potatoes, onions, and sauce on the side.

# CHRISTMAS QUICHE

### SERVES 4–6

One of my favorite things about Christmas meals in France is the chestnuts (*châtaignes*, in French). I grew up with horse chestnut trees in my neighborhood, but I didn't discover edible chestnuts until arriving in Burgundy.

In France, chestnuts and festive turkeys go hand in hand. Turkey stuffing is based around ground meat and chestnuts instead of cubed bread. Chestnuts can also be warmed and served along with the turkey. There's not much of a recipe in there: warm them, serve them!

However, I love this festive-feeling tart, packed full of delicious winter flavors. It's perfect for Christmas Eve or Boxing Day. You can find unpeeled chestnuts in most grocery stores at that time of year and can generally find peeled chestnuts (far easier to use) in either canned or Tetra Pak form as well.

Got your chestnuts? Here we go!

---

Heat the oven to 400°F.

On a lightly floured surface, roll out the dough to a circle about ⅛-inch thick and large enough to cover the bottom and sides of a 9½-inch tart pan. Roll it around your rolling pin, then unroll it into the pan, tucking the dough into all the sides. Trim the top so it sits about ¼ inch higher than the edge of the pan. Poke the bottom of the pastry all over with a fork so it doesn't puff up.

Cut out a 10-inch round of parchment paper and place it inside the pan, on top of the dough. Fill the pan with baking beads or dry beans. Bake until the pastry is browned, 20–25 minutes. Remove the beads and parchment. Turn down the oven to 350°F.

Place a large sauté pan over medium heat and melt 1 Tbsp of the butter. Add the onions and cook, stirring, until softened, about 5 minutes. Add the remaining 1 Tbsp butter. Add the mushrooms and cook until they are browned and have released their liquid, 10–12 minutes. Add the garlic and cook for another 30 seconds. Add the wine and cook until most of the liquid has cooked off, but the mixture is not dry, 3–5 minutes. Stir in the thyme and season with sea salt and pepper.

Add the mushroom mixture to the tart shell and scatter the chestnuts evenly over top.

In a small bowl, whisk together the cream and egg until well mixed. Pour this over the chestnuts.

Scatter the goat cheese evenly over top.

Bake until the center of the quiche no longer jiggles, 25–35 minutes. Let sit for 10 minutes before serving.

½ recipe Marie's French Pastry (page 39)

2 Tbsp butter, divided

½ small onion, minced

4 cups sliced mushrooms, such as cremini, oyster, or shiitake

2 cloves garlic, minced

¼ cup dry white wine

1 tsp fresh thyme leaves

¾ cup jarred or canned prepared chestnuts, quartered

½ cup heavy cream

1 egg

4 oz plain goat cheese

# CREAMY DIJON CHICKEN
## with Bacon and Spinach

### SERVES 4–6

Anything with a hearty dose of Dijon mustard in it feels like Burgundy to me. This recipe includes a spin on an everyday sauce I was taught by my first host mother. It makes everything taste good. After cooking a steak or turkey fillet—really, any meat or poultry—remove the meat and stir a tablespoon of Dijon into the browned bits left in the pan. When well mixed, add crème fraîche until the sauce is your desired consistency and mix well.

Rebecca has taken this basic sauce, replaced the crème fraîche with heavy cream, and dressed it up beautifully with bacon (what the French call *lardons*) and spinach so it is fancy enough to impress even the snootiest guest—though I'm hoping you don't invite that type of person to your house often, because nothing ruins a dinner like pretentious company.

In a large, heavy-bottomed pot over medium heat, cook the bacon until browned and the fat has been rendered, about 10 minutes. Using a slotted spoon, transfer the bacon to a large platter. Keep about 1 Tbsp of bacon fat in the pot and discard the rest.

Season the chicken on all sides with kosher salt and pepper.

Add the chicken to the pot and brown it on all sides, about 15 minutes. Don't worry if it's not cooked all the way through, as it will finish in the sauce. Transfer the chicken to the platter with the bacon.

Leave about 1 Tbsp fat in the pot again. Cook the onions until browned and softened, about 10 minutes. Add the garlic and cook for another 2 minutes. Add the wine and deglaze the pot, scraping up all the brown bits off the bottom. Add the stock, whisk in the cream and Dijon, add the tomatoes, and season with salt and pepper.

Bring to a soft boil, then turn down the heat to medium-low. Return the bacon and chicken to the pot and simmer, uncovered, until the chicken is cooked through and the sauce has thickened a bit, about 25 minutes.

Stir in the spinach and cook until it is wilted, about 3 minutes. Stir in the thyme and lemon juice and serve with rice, pasta, or potatoes.

½ lb thick-cut bacon, sliced crosswise into ½-inch pieces

8 boneless chicken thighs, skin on

2 onions, julienned

3 large garlic cloves, minced

1 cup dry white wine

1 cup Chicken Stock (page 26 or store-bought)

½ cup heavy cream

2 Tbsp grainy Dijon mustard

1 large tomato, diced

4 cups baby spinach leaves

1 Tbsp thyme leaves

2 Tbsp lemon juice

# STEAK WITH PEPPER SAUCE

**SERVES 2**

This is another recipe Alain, our Renaissance man window-installation expert at La Maison des Deux Clochers, taught me. I was cooking up steaks for lunch in the midst of the drywall dust and renovation detritus, and Alain came in and methodically instructed me step-by-step through a wine and pepper sauce to pour over top. I wanted to murder him at the time, as I was really *not* in the mood to be learning new recipes.

However, all was forgiven when I took a bite of the steak covered in this rich, deep sauce. Alain advised pairing it with a dry red wine (preferably from the Côte de Nuits).

---

Place a large sauté pan over medium heat and melt the butter.

Add the shallot and cook until softened, 2–3 minutes.

Add the peppercorns, wine, and cognac (or brandy or marsala). Simmer to reduce the liquid by about one quarter, 4–5 minutes.

Whisk in the stock and Dijon. Simmer until the sauce has reduced enough to coat the back of a spoon, 5–7 minutes.

Stir in the cream and then the pepper. Season to taste with sea salt. Remove from the heat and keep covered while you cook the steaks.

Serve with boiled baby potatoes and braised spinach, pouring the sauce over the sliced steaks.

1 Tbsp butter

1 small shallot, finely minced

2 Tbsp jarred green peppercorns (the kind in liquid, not dry)

¼ cup dry white wine

2 Tbsp cognac or brandy or marsala

¼ cup Beef Stock (page 25 or store-bought)

2 tsp Dijon mustard

¼ cup whipping cream

1 tsp freshly ground pepper (black works great, but a combo of white, red, and black peppercorns is even better)

2 of your favorite steaks

# BRAISED ENDIVES
## with Ham and Béchamel

SERVES 8

This may sound like an odd combination, but it is still, twenty-five-plus years after I first tried it, one of my favorite meals. For me, this dish is comfort food incarnate. Warm, satisfying, and creamy, it has it all.

This was a specialty of my third host mother in Nuits-Saint-Georges. The first time she served it as the main course at one of our formal lunches in the grand dining room of the family manor, where her pharmacist husband held forth with spontaneous lectures on the state of the world, I was skeptical.

After my first bite, though, I knew I had found (yet another) new favorite. I make these often during the winter, and my family love them as much as I do. Also, it's a wonderful way to introduce *les pétits* to the glory of the humble endive. My favorite thing is to have one in the fridge that I reheat for lunch. Those *pétits bonheurs du jour* make life joyous, even in the dark days of January.

3 Tbsp butter

8 large Belgian endives, root end removed but otherwise left whole

8 slices cooked ham (see note)

1 recipe Béchamel Sauce (page 29)

1 cup grated Gruyère or Emmenthal cheese

Heat the oven to 375°F.

Set a large sauté pan over medium-low heat and melt the butter. Add the endives and braise, rotating every 3–4 minutes, until nicely browned on all sides, about 30 minutes in total. Remove from the heat.

Wrap each endive in a slice of ham and place in a casserole dish that will fit them all without crowding, seam-side down.

Pour the béchamel evenly over top and then sprinkle with the cheese.

Bake until warmed through and the cheese is bubbling, 30–40 minutes. Set the oven to broil for the last 5 minutes of baking. Let it rest for 15 minutes before serving.

*It's important to use the right type of ham for this recipe. When I'm in France, I use jambon blanc; when I'm in North America, I use prosciutto cotto. This will give you a nice neutral flavor that lets the endives and béchamel take center stage. You don't want to use smoked or seasoned ham for this (for example, the Black Forest or rosemary ham you find at deli counters), as the flavors intensify during cooking and overpower the other flavors.* —LB

# THE CHEESE PLATTER

In France, cheese is a course in its own right and comes between the main course and the dessert (see page 187). I could wax rhapsodic about this simple fact for days, but I will spare you and instead get down to the nitty gritty of how to compose a wonderful cheese board.

Five cheeses is a good number to start with. I always prefer odd numbers to even numbers when assembling a cheese platter—it just looks better somehow. Here are some types of cheeses you can add.

*A medium to hard sheep cheese such as a Manchego or a Lévéjac (pictured is a Tomme)*

*A blue cheese such as a Roquefort (pictured) or a Stilton*

*A goat cheese such as Selles-sur-Cher (pictured) or Saint-Maure*

Each region in France has its specialty cheeses. The French take pride in their incredible wealth of cheese (and so they should!) and often boast that there is a different cheese in France for every day of the year. In truth, there are far more cheeses than that, and one of my favorite things when traveling to a different region in France is trying their specialty cheeses.

Here in North America a cheese board usually includes many things besides cheese—crackers, olives, cured meats, grapes... The French are generally far more minimalist when it comes to the presentation of cheese. A cheese course in France is just that: a variety of cheeses to choose from. Baguette slices are usually on the table anyway in a separate bowl or basket. *Facile!*

I always serve cheeses whole, as that is the way I learned to do it in France. To serve just a portion of a freshly bought cheese feels a bit cheap to me. Then again, Franck and I are a running joke among our friends for always providing ten times the food our guests could possibly eat. I guess this habit has to do with the fact that cheese is so much less expensive and more plentiful in France. Of course, it is

*A soft cow cheese such as a Camembert (pictured) or Brie*

*A hard cow cheese such as a Comté (pictured) or an excellent cheddar*

perfectly acceptable to serve some partially consumed cheeses on a cheeseboard, although maybe not at a formal dinner.

Wrap cheese in wax or butcher's paper to store it—never in plastic wrap. I always take it out of the fridge an hour before serving to bring it up to room temperature, which is the ideal serving condition for all cheeses.

Besides bread, we were rather stumped when it came to finding enough side recipes for this cookbook. Because we eat a series of smaller courses in France, sides aren't as automatically included in a meal as they are in North America. The most popular sides—in Burgundy at least—tend to be of the starchy variety: potatoes in their many forms (dauphinois, mashed, boiled with butter and parsley), egg noodles, or even rice. These all have something in common: they do an excellent job of soaking up yummy sauces. Having said that, if you are looking for a stellar side dish, here are some wonderful French ideas.

# ON THE SIDE

# FRENCH BREAD

## MAKES 1 LARGE LOAF

It may seem rather odd to see bread included with the other side dishes in this book. While baguettes and country loaves may not be considered as sides per se, I challenge you to experience a French meal that does not include a hunk of bread on the side of your plate. Go ahead. I dare you. Bread is used as a fork, a sauce soaker, and a cheese conveyer. *Tu vois?* In France, it is actually the quintessential side. (Insider tip: it is generally not served with butter and asking for butter is viewed as rather strange.)

I went berserk for it when I arrived in France (who doesn't?). In the weeks before my school year started, I would trot to the village *boulangerie* in Nuits-Saint-Georges with my host mother and buy the daily quota of fresh baguettes (generally half a baguette per person). On our way home, we would sneak a ripped-off piece from the end of the baguettes and enjoy the airy, chewy bread as we walked home over the cobblestones.

When we don't have bread with a meal Franck becomes frantic. For him, and so many other French people, a meal just isn't a meal without bread.

Baguettes can be difficult to shape without proper molds, so a beautiful round country loaf is often easiest for the home cook. The true beauty of French bread lies in its simplicity: water, flour, salt, and yeast. Nothing else is needed. Nothing else is desired.

1 (8 g) envelope of instant dry yeast

3½ cups all-purpose flour

2 tsp kosher salt

Vegetable oil for greasing bowl

---

In a small bowl, pour the yeast over 1½ cups warm water (105°F is ideal) and stir. Let sit until the mixture begins to form bubbles, indicating that the yeast is active, about 10 minutes. If the mixture doesn't bubble, discard it and start again with fresh yeast.

Place the flour and salt in a stand mixer fitted with the whisk attachment and whisk on the lowest speed to blend. Pour in the yeast mixture, attach the dough hook, and mix on low speed until a ball forms and the dough is pulling away from the sides, about 2 minutes. Use a rubber spatula to scrape down the sides as you go. If the dough is too wet, add flour 1 Tbsp at a time, until the dough is soft but not sticky.

Stop the mixer and let the dough rest for 2 minutes.

Knead again on low speed for 5 minutes. Stop the mixer and press into the dough with your thumb. If the dough springs back, it is done. If not, knead for another 2 minutes.

Spray or brush a large bowl lightly with a neutral-flavored oil. Flip the dough onto a lightly floured surface and knead manually for 2 minutes. Place the dough in the oiled bowl and cover with plastic, then a tea towel. Let sit in a warm, draft-free spot until tripled in size, 2–3 hours.

Flip the dough out onto a lightly floured surface and flatten slightly into a square. If the dough feels too wet, knead in 1 Tbsp of flour. Pull the bottom left-

hand corner over onto the top right-hand corner, then pull the bottom right-hand corner over onto the top left-hand corner. Repeat this a few more times with each corner of what's now a triangle. Finally, pull the corners of the dough down and under, rounding the top into a ball. Place in the oiled bowl again and cover with plastic and a tea towel. Let sit in a warm spot until tripled in size again, about 1 hour this time.

Line a large rimmed sheet pan with parchment paper.

Flip the dough out onto a lightly floured surface again and flatten slightly. Using both hands, start turning the dough under, forming a ball and stretching the top "skin" to form a round. Bring the stretched dough together underneath and pinch to seal. Place it on the parchment and cover with the same bowl you were using before. Let rise in a warm, draft-free spot until about triple in size again, about 90 minutes this time around.

Set the oven rack in the center position and heat the oven to 450°F. On the bottom rack, set a large rimmed pan filled with about 2 cups of water. Allow the oven to heat for a good ½ hour.

When you are ready to bake, use a sharp knife to make a large X, about ¼-inch deep in the top of the bread, and brush the dough liberally with water.

Bake for 3 minutes. Remove from the oven and spray or brush liberally with water again. Return to the oven and bake for another 3 minutes. Ensure there is still at least 1 cup of water in the bottom pan. Bake for 3 more minutes then remove from the oven and spray or brush with water. Return to the oven and bake until the bread is nicely browned and the top is crusty, 25–30 minutes.

Remove from the oven and let rest on a cooling rack for about 1 hour before slicing. Of course, there is nothing better than bread fresh from the oven, but if you wrap the uncut portion of the loaf in plastic wrap, it will keep for a day or two, after which time it is best turned into toast.

*I've made lots of types of bread over the years, but for a classic French loaf, I turned to the master, Julia Child. What makes this bread so delicious is the repeated rising times that allow the flavors to develop deeply and the multiple doses of water at the beginning of baking, which gives the bread a lovely, crispy, brown crust. It is hard to believe that such a simple combination of water, flour, yeast, and salt can make such a satisfying and hearty loaf, but it does indeed.—RW*

# ROASTED GREEN VEG
## *with Lemon and Tarragon*

SERVES 4–6

This recipe is a beautiful mix of some of my favorite French flavors: tarragon, lemon, leeks, and asparagus. It's beautiful as a side for lunch or even an entrée in its own right. Best eaten, I think, on a warm spring day in the dappled shade of a wisteria climbing an old stone wall.

Heat the oven to 425°F. Line two large rimmed sheet pans with parchment paper.

Toss the broccoli, leeks, and asparagus with the oil and season liberally with sea salt and pepper. Spread across the sheet pans and roast until the vegetables have softened a bit and are slightly browned, 15–20 minutes. Give them a toss at the 10-minute point.

If at the 15-minute point the vegetables are starting to brown, sprinkle minced garlic over them for the last 5 minutes of roasting. If they are not starting to brown yet, roast for another 5 minutes before adding the garlic and roasting for an additional 5 minutes.

Boil the peas in a small pot over medium heat until just tender, 3–5 minutes. Drain. Add the butter and lemon juice and stir until the butter is melted. Add the tarragon and lemon zest. Season with salt and pepper.

Arrange the broccoli, leeks, and asparagus in a serving bowl. Pour the pea mixture over top and toss to coat all the vegetables with the butter and herbs. Garnish with edible flowers and snap peas (if using).

6 cups broccoli florets

2 leeks, white and light-green parts only, sliced into ¼-inch rounds

½ lb slim asparagus, tough bottoms trimmed

3 Tbsp olive oil

1 large garlic clove, finely minced

1 cup fresh or frozen green peas

2 Tbsp butter

2 tsp lemon juice

2 Tbsp fresh tarragon leaves

2 tsp grated lemon zest

Edible flowers such as chives (optional)

Sugar snap peas for garnish (optional)

*Keeping vegetables on the baking sheet in a single layer and not too close together will prevent them from steaming and will instead give them a bit of crispiness and brown color. The best way to serve roasted veg!—RW*

# WARM LENTILS À LA LYONNAISE

## SERVES 6 AS A SIDE OR 4 AS A MAIN

I found in France there was so much more scope for cooking and eating lentils, one of my favorite foods. For a quick salad at lunch, Franck and I would often throw cooked du Puy lentils in with a homemade vinaigrette and any vegetables or crumbly cheese (such as feta) we had in the fridge.

My favorite lentil dishes are served warm, and are inspired by our neighbor to the south, the beautiful city of Lyon (a UNESCO world-heritage site, like our wine coast in Burgundy). Lyon knows lentils, and this is their take on them. For me, this is yet another comfort dish. You can serve them warm with almost any meat, or by themselves with a poached or fried egg on top for a light dinner.

---

Place the lentils in a medium pot and fill it with cold water. Add the bay leaves. Bring to a boil and cook, stirring occasionally, until the lentils are soft enough to bite through but still firm and not mushy, 25–35 minutes.

Drain and remove the bay leaves. Pour the lentils into a large bowl.

Add the desired amount of dressing to the lentils while they are still warm. Start with ½ cup of the dressing, then taste and add more if desired.

Stir in the bacon, scallions, and parsley and season with sea salt and pepper.

Spoon into a serving bowl if serving as a side, or onto individual plates if serving as a main, and add poached or fried eggs if desired.

1½ cups Puy lentils, rinsed

2 bay leaves

Mme Beaupré's Homemade Vinaigrette (page 21)

6 cooked strips of bacon, chopped

¼ cup finely chopped scallions

¼ cup minced parsley

Poached or fried eggs (optional) for as many people as you are serving

# FRENCH ONION RICE PILAF

### SERVES 4

I don't know about you, but I cannot get enough of the flavors in that culinary classic French onion soup (page 79). Soup is an entrée in its own right, so Rebecca has taken those flavors and created this side of delicious pilaf, which goes brilliantly with myriad dishes and brings back that cozy, heartwarming hug of onions, white wine, and garlic. This is a dish that you will find yourself using on repeat.

1 Tbsp olive oil

1 large onion, halved and thinly sliced

¼ cup dry white wine

1 small garlic clove, minced

1 cup long-grain white rice

1 tsp sea salt

1¾ cups Chicken Stock (page 26) or Beef Stock (page 25 or store-bought)

1 Tbsp butter, cubed

½ cup minced parsley

Set a medium heavy-bottomed pot over medium-high heat. Add the oil and then the onions and cook, stirring, until softened, about 10 minutes. Add the wine and cook for another 8 minutes, scraping up any brown bits from the bottom of the pot. Add the garlic and cook for another minute, then add the rice and salt, stirring well to coat the rice with the onion mixture.

Pour in the stock and bring to a boil. Turn down the heat, cover, and simmer until the rice is cooked and the liquid has been absorbed, 15 minutes.

Remove from the heat and let sit for 10 minutes.

Stir in the butter and then the parsley and serve.

# CAULIFLOWER GRATIN
## with Garlic and Sage

### SERVES 6–8

One sterling exception to the general French indifference to side dishes is vegetable gratins. These are cooked vegetables with a homemade béchamel-based sauce poured over top, and sometimes topped with cheese before broiling in the oven to make a beautiful golden crust.

Rebecca has taken an old standby of mine, a humble cauliflower gratin, and created this incredible taste combination. Garlic and sage marry beautifully with the delicate taste of the cauliflower and the creamy sauce. This can also be served as a lovely main dish and the leftovers. . . I guarantee they won't last long.

2 Tbsp olive oil, divided

1 small onion, julienned

4 cloves garlic, minced

1 large head of cauliflower, chopped into 1–2-inch florets

¾ cup Chicken Stock (page 26 or store-bought)

3 Tbsp butter

¼ cup all-purpose flour

2 cups heavy cream

½ tsp freshly grated nutmeg

½ cup sage leaves, julienned, divided

2½ cups grated Gruyère cheese, divided

1 tsp Dijon mustard

¼ cup fine fresh breadcrumbs

Heat the oven to 375°F. Grease a 12-inch cast iron pan or a 9- x 13-inch casserole dish with 1 Tbsp of the oil and set aside.

Place a large pot over medium heat and add the remaining 1 Tbsp oil. Add the onions and sauté until softened, 5–7 minutes. Add the garlic and sauté for another minute. Add the cauliflower and stock. Bring to a boil, cover, and steam until cauliflower is fork-tender, 10–12 minutes.

While the cauliflower is steaming, make the cheese sauce. Place a large saucepan over medium heat and melt the butter. Whisk in the flour and continue whisking for about 3 minutes, until the mixture is slightly browned. Continue to whisk as you add the cream. Increase the heat to high. As soon as the mixture reaches a boil, remove from the heat and whisk in the nutmeg. Stir in ¼ cup of the sage and then 1 cup of the cheese. Taste and season with sea salt and pepper. Pour the sauce evenly over cauliflower and stir in the Dijon to combine.

Once the cauliflower is cooked, remove the lid of the pot to let the steam escape. Season to taste with sea salt and pepper. Using a slotted spoon, transfer the cauliflower into the prepared pan (or casserole dish), shaking off any residual liquid.

Sprinkle the cauliflower evenly with the remaining ¼ cup sage, remaining 1½ cups of cheese, and the breadcrumbs.

Bake, uncovered, until the cauliflower is very tender and cheese is bubbly and brown, about 30 minutes. Let sit for 5 minutes before serving.

*A great fall dish, this goes perfectly with roast chicken and is a nice substitute for potatoes or even a stand-in for good old mac 'n' cheese! If you're looking for a little extra something, stir some cooked bacon into the cheese sauce before combining with the cauliflower. —RW*

# ROASTED SQUASH WITH GARLIC

## SERVES 4–6

Squash are lifesavers in the winter, when the choice of other fruits and vegetables starts thinning out at our local markets in France. Squash is just so darn *wholesome*—it's what a friend of mine calls a "huggy" food. It goes well with pretty much any kind of protein and adds not only color to the plate—which is important in France, where good-looking food is always appreciated—but also nutrition and deliciousness to your meal.

1 large acorn squash

2 Tbsp olive oil

4 Tbsp butter, divided

2 large cloves garlic, finely minced

1 Tbsp minced fresh oregano leaves

1 Tbsp lemon juice

Heat the oven to 450°F. Line a large rimmed sheet pan with parchment paper.

Cut the bottom off the squash to make a flat surface. Set the squash on its now-flat bottom and, using a very sharp knife, carefully cut it into six to eight wedges and scrape out the seeds with a spoon.

Coat each wedge with olive oil and season with sea salt and pepper. Place the wedges on the prepared sheet pan, one side of the flesh down, and roast until nicely browned, 20 minutes. Flip each wedge and roast until fork-tender and nicely browned on this side as well, 10–15 minutes.

While the squash is roasting, make the sauce. In a medium saucepan over medium heat, melt 3 Tbsp of the butter. Turn down the heat to medium-low and add the garlic. Cook, stirring, until the garlic is softened, but not browned, about 10 minutes. Turn down the heat if necessary, to avoid burning. Remove from the heat, then stir in the remaining 1 Tbsp butter, the oregano, and the lemon juice, and season with salt and pepper.

Place the wedges on a serving platter and drizzle them with the sauce. Serve immediately.

# FRENCH GREEN BEANS
## with Crispy Shallots

SERVES 4–6

Green beans were yet another thing I never considered a favorite before living in France. The few specimens I had been forced to gag down back home were usually boiled to within an inch of their lives and served with, at most, a pat of butter.

When I illicitly moved into Franck's house at the very end of my exchange year in France (it created quite the *scandale*, but you can read about that in *My Grape Year*), Franck's parents would often have a dinner of just green beans and a small bit of meat, always with a gorgeous sauce. I watched in stupefaction as Franck and his sister Stéphanie served themselves great mountains of green beans—that is, until I tried them myself. For one thing, French green beans are superior to your average North American green bean, so definitely make the extra effort to locate some of those. They are crispier and longer, and hold their shape.

It dawned on me that French green beans were delicious. In France, they counted as a comfort food. Franck's family would add a dollop of Dijon mustard and mix it up in their green beans, which adds a spiky flavor that all of a sudden makes them far more interesting than I could have imagined. Rebecca's addition of crispy shallots in this recipe, elevates green beans to the sublime.

1 lb long green beans, washed and trimmed

1 Tbsp butter

5 large shallots, cut into thin rings

1 large garlic clove, minced

2 tsp grated lemon zest

2 Tbsp lemon juice

2 Tbsp heavy cream

---

Bring a large pot of salted water to a boil and add the beans. Cook for 5 minutes, then rinse thoroughly under cold, running water to stop the cooking. Set aside.

Warm a large skillet over medium heat and melt the butter. Add the shallots and cook, stirring, until browned and softened, 10–12 minutes. Add the garlic and cook for another 2 minutes, stirring frequently so the garlic doesn't burn.

Increase the heat to medium-high, add the beans to the skillet, and cook, stirring regularly, until the beans are browned a bit and the shallots are crispy, 5–7 minutes. Add the lemon zest, lemon juice, and cream. Stir to combine and cook for another 1–2 minutes. Season generously with sea salt and pepper.

# MAPLE-DIJON ROASTED CARROTS

**SERVES 6**

In my experience, as I mentioned earlier, sides in Burgundy (when they come at all) often tend to come in the form of the humble potato in all of its glorious forms—or green beans. However, I mentioned to Rebecca that glazed carrots did appear with some frequency and were always delicious.

As you can see in this recipe, Rebecca took this simple idea and ran with it, creating a Franco-Canadian fusion dish that combines carrots, Dijon mustard, and maple syrup. When I tasted this recipe I instantly decided it would become part of my repertoire. It also adds a lovely note of color to your plate.

Heat the oven to 400°F. Line a large rimmed sheet pan with parchment paper.

Scrub, rinse, and dry the carrots. Place them in a medium bowl, toss with the oil, and season well with sea salt and pepper. Lay them on the sheet pan, taking care not to crowd them too much. (Use two sheet pans if necessary.) Roast, turning occasionally, until lightly browned on all sides and cooked through, 30–40 minutes.

In the meantime, in a small saucepan over medium heat, combine the butter, maple syrup, Dijon, and quatre épices. Whisk to blend and stir to heat through, about 5 minutes, then remove from the heat. Stir in 2 tsp of the thyme.

Place the cooked carrots on a serving platter, and pour the maple-Dijon sauce over top. Sprinkle with the remaining 1 tsp thyme and serve immediately.

2 lb carrots

2 Tbsp extra virgin olive oil

3 Tbsp unsalted butter

3 Tbsp grade A maple syrup

2½ Tbsp grainy Dijon mustard

2 tsp Quatre Épices (page 19)

3 tsp thyme leaves, divided

# TIAN DE LÉGUMES

## SERVES 8–10

I picked up on this classic French vegetable dish that hails from Provence soon after moving to Burgundy. It's so easy to assemble and so delicious with the plentiful *légumes de soleil* (literally, "vegetables of sun"). I cannot even begin to explain how well this goes down on a warm summer evening with a glass of rosé.

We often added rounds of fresh mozzarella into the mix, skipped the breadcrumbs and Parmesan, and made it our main course for a summer evening meal. Try this and you will be eating it all summer long. (For best results, keep the vegetables as close in size and circumference as possible.)

---

Heat the oven to 400°F. Rub a 2½-quart casserole dish, or a deep 10-inch cast iron pan, with the 1 Tbsp oil. Round, oval, or square vessels all work well. The dish just needs to be deep enough to hold the vegetables standing up on their sides.

Heat a large frying pan over medium heat. Melt the butter and then add the onions. Sauté until the onions are softened and slightly browned, about 10 minutes. Add the garlic and sauté for another minute. Add the wine and scrape the pan to scoop up any flavorful brown bits from the bottom. Cook to meld the flavors, another 3 minutes, then spoon the mixture into the prepared dish (or pan).

Using a sharp knife or a mandoline, slice the zucchinis, eggplants, and tomatoes into ¼-inch rounds. Season all the pieces with sea salt and pepper. Arrange the rounds in the dish (or pan), stacking them upright, in a circular pattern, and alternating vegetables. So: zucchini, eggplant, tomato, repeat, until the entire dish is full. Tuck them in there good and tight.

Combine the ⅓ cup oil, all the fresh or dried herbs, and some salt and pepper in a small bowl. Pour this over the vegetables.

Cover tightly with aluminum foil and bake for 30 minutes. Remove the foil and bake for another 20 minutes. This will allow some of the juice to steam away so the vegetables don't boil.

Sprinkle the breadcrumbs and cheese over top. Return to the oven until the topping is browned and bubbly, 15 minutes.

### Ingredients

⅓ cup olive oil + 1 Tbsp for oiling the casserole dish

2 Tbsp butter

2 small onions, minced

2 large cloves of garlic, minced

2 Tbsp dry white wine

2 large zucchinis or summer squash (a combo of yellow and green is good)

2 eggplants

3 large tomatoes

2 Tbsp dried herbes de Provence (page 20), or 4 Tbsp fresh herbs, such as thyme, rosemary, savory, parsley, and lavender

½ cup panko breadcrumbs

½ cup grated Parmesan or pecorino cheese

---

*There is a fine line between a tian and a ratatouille in French cuisine, and they are often confused for one another. Tian is thinly sliced vegetables, arranged in a fancy pattern, over a sauce or base of sorts. Ratatouille is more of a stew, though both dishes contain very similar vegetables. I've taken a certain liberty by adding a gratin with the breadcrumbs and Parmesan; however, this is completely optional. The onions, garlic, and herbs add such a nice flavor to the vegetables on their own, though I do appreciate a bit of a crispy crust on top to add more texture. —RW*

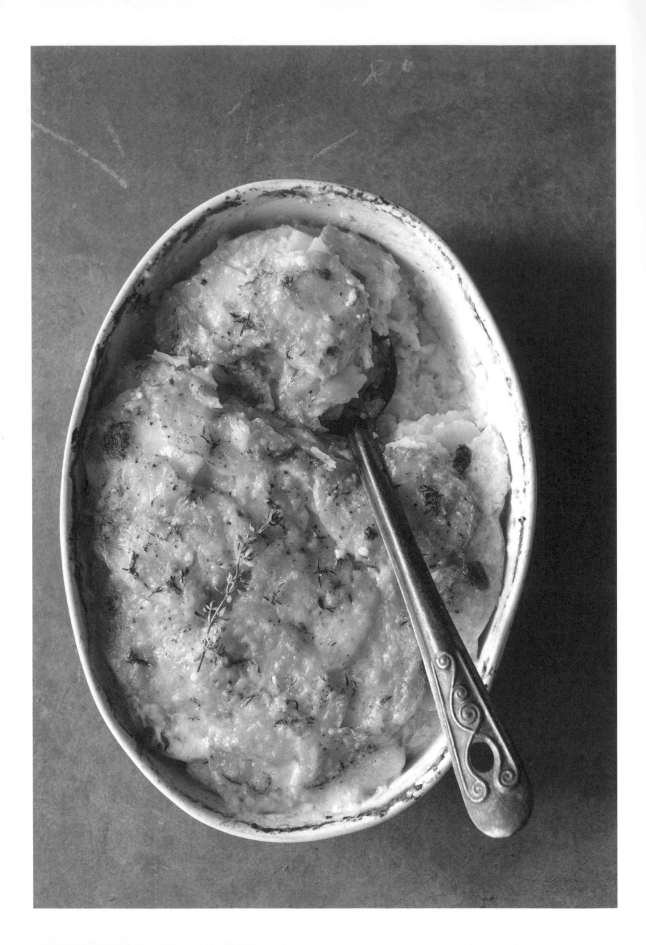

# GRATIN DAUPHINOIS

Burgundians really love potatoes, and my husband is no exception. In my opinion, he also makes the world's best gratin dauphinois, that basic but beautiful French side dish. His version is remarkably simple and eschews the layers of gunky cheese that often typify the North American version of scalloped potatoes.

His secret is extremely finely sliced potatoes—use a mandoline if you have one (but careful with your fingertips!). Thin slices soak up the sauce perfectly and look exquisite when layered. Gratin dauphinois goes perfectly with those two other icons of French cooking, boeuf bourguignon (page 117) and coq au vin (page 121), but is so versatile that it goes beautifully with many other things as well.

4 lb white or yellow potatoes, peeled (or scrubbed if peel isn't too thick)

1½ cups whipping cream

2 Tbsp melted butter

2 cloves of garlic, minced

¼ tsp freshly ground nutmeg

3 tsp thyme leaves, divided

Heat the oven to 375°F. Lightly butter a 9- x 13-inch casserole dish, at least 3 inches tall. Set aside.

Slice the potatoes as thinly as you can, with a mandoline if you have one. The thinner the better, so all the flavors cook through.

In a large measuring cup, stir together the cream and butter, then stir in the garlic and nutmeg. Season with sea salt and pepper.

Lay one third of the potato slices in the bottom of the casserole, salting lightly as you go. (Potatoes can take it!) Press them down as you layer.

Pour one third of the cream mixture over the potatoes. Sprinkle 1 tsp of the thyme over top and season with pepper.

Repeat with another layer of potatoes, cream, and thyme. Lay out one more layer of potatoes and cream. If the casserole is very full, place it on a parchment-lined, rimmed sheet pan in case it bubbles over a bit.

Cover the casserole tightly with aluminum foil. Bake for 75 minutes. At this point, prick the potatoes in the center to see if they are tender. If so, remove the foil and bake until the top is browned, 15–20 minutes. If not, cook covered with the foil for another 10 minutes, then remove the foil to brown the top.

Let rest for 10 minutes before serving.

# WHITE BEANS
## *with Garlic and Rosemary*

SERVES 4–6

Franck's parents always make this side dish when they serve a roasted leg of lamb with olive oil and herbes de Provence. I love lamb, but it is the white beans that have me reaching for seconds and sometimes even thirds. This creamy concoction with garlic and rosemary hits every satisfying note for me. At our homes in both Burgundy and here in Victoria we have huge rosemary bushes outside our front doors—they are wonderful for neglectful gardeners like me—so it is easy to step out and snip off a fresh stalk. Whenever there are beans left over, I heat them up for my lunch or dinner and savor every hearty bite.

½ cup fruity olive oil

3 (each 6 inches) stalks of rosemary, divided

2 large garlic cloves, peeled and smashed

2 (each 19 oz) cans of white kidney (cannellini) beans

2 tsp grated lemon zest

2 Tbsp lemon juice

1 cup cherry tomatoes, halved

Place a small saucepan over medium-low heat and add the oil. Add 2 of the rosemary stalks and the garlic. Watching closely, bring the oil *just* to a simmer. You will hear the rosemary and garlic sizzle. As soon as the oil comes to a simmer, remove from the heat and set aside. Allow the rosemary and garlic to infuse the oil for at least 30 minutes and up to 3 hours.

Drain and rinse the beans. Place them in a large bowl. Remove the garlic and rosemary from the oil and pour the oil over the beans. Pull the leaves from the 2 rosemary stalks plus the third reserved stalk and mince. Add the garlic cloves and a pinch of kosher salt to the rosemary and continue to mince the mixture together until a chunky sort of paste forms. Stir this into the beans and oil mixture.

Add the lemon zest and juice to the beans, followed by the tomatoes. Season generously with salt and pepper. Serve as is, or heat in a pot over low heat for a warm alternative.

# BRAISED BABY ONIONS

I have a bit of an obsession with miniature things, whether it be those tiny sample-sized Bonne Maman jam jars, espresso cups, or onions. In France, there are always a few pickled pearl onions in the jar of cornichons, and I never let any of them go to waste.

Rebecca has created a phenomenal side dish here that capitalizes on the miniature gorgeousness of tiny onions, braised in cognac and stock. It's a beautiful and scrumptious side that would marry beautifully with any sort of meat.

1½ lb pearl or cipollini onions

2 Tbsp butter

2 Tbsp extra virgin olive oil

1 Tbsp brandy or cognac

2 bay leaves

½ cup Chicken Stock (page 26) or Beef Stock (page 25 or store-bought)

2 tsp fresh thyme leaves

Set a large pot full of water over high heat and bring to a boil. Add the onions and boil for 30 seconds. Using a slotted spoon, remove the onions from the pot and rinse well under cold, running water to stop the cooking. Peel all the onions (the blanching will make this easier) and, if you're using cipollinis, cut them in half if they are bigger than a couple of inches in diameter.

Set a large sauté pan (one with a lid) over medium heat, melt the butter, and swirl in the oil. Add the onions and sauté, stirring regularly, being careful not to break them apart, until they start to get some color to them, about 10 minutes. Stir in the brandy (or cognac). Add the bay leaves and stock, cover, turn down the heat to low, and simmer until the onions are softened and the liquid has mostly evaporated, about 30 minutes. Remove from the heat, stir in the thyme, and let sit, uncovered, for about 10 minutes. Season with sea salt and pepper and serve.

# SPINACH SOUFFLÉ

## SERVES 6

What do you think of when you think of French cuisine? Soufflé probably is not far from your mind, *n'est-ce pas*? Soufflé can be a main course, but it also makes a spectacular side dish. When I first arrived in France, I thought soufflés took some sort of unattainable culinary skill to master. I figured it was the sort of thing you had to be born French to figure out (rather like how to get clean in a bathtub with a handheld shower nozzle—something I still can't do without turning the bathroom into Niagara Falls). I quickly realized, however, that soufflés are not impossible for me, especially this recipe. The instructions are fairly foolproof (or, Laura-proof as I like to say) as well as giving a huge return for my cooking effort. If only showering in a bathtub were this easy.

Heat the oven to 400°F. Butter six 8 oz ramekins and place them on a large rimmed baking sheet.

In a pot over medium heat, melt the butter. Add the shallot and cook until softened, about 2 minutes. Add the thyme and parsley and cook, stirring, for about 1 minute more. Sprinkle in the flour and, whisking constantly, cook until light golden, 2–3 minutes. In a slow, steady stream, whisk in the milk until the mixture is smooth. Bring to a boil, turn down the heat to a simmer, and cook, whisking constantly, as the mixture thickens, about 5 minutes. Stir in the nutmeg and season with sea salt and pepper. Remove from the heat and let cool for about 15 minutes. The mixture will continue to thicken into the consistency of thick pudding.

In a large bowl, whisk together the egg yolks. Add about ¼ cup of the milk mixture, whisking constantly. Add another ¼ cup, whisking again, and then whisk in the remaining milk mixture. Fold in the spinach, cheese, salt, and pepper to taste.

In a large bowl, using an electric mixer on high speed, beat the egg whites with the cream of tartar until medium-firm peaks form, 1–2 minutes. Fold one third of the whites into the spinach mixture, then fold in the rest of the whites until well blended. Divide the mixture evenly between the prepared ramekins. Bake until puffed and golden on top, about 30 minutes. Do not open the oven until 30 minutes have passed, or the soufflés might fall! Serve immediately with a simple, citrusy salad.

3 Tbsp butter, plus softened butter for greasing

2½ tsp finely minced shallot

2 tsp finely minced thyme leaves

1 tsp finely minced parsley

3 Tbsp all-purpose flour

1¼ cups whole milk

Pinch freshly grated nutmeg

4 large egg yolks

2 boxes (each 10 oz) frozen spinach, thawed, squeezed dry, and finely chopped

½ cup shredded Gruyère or Emmenthal cheese

½ tsp sea salt

4 large egg whites

¼ tsp cream of tartar

When I looked at my list of proposed recipes for this book, I wasn't surprised to see that the majority of them were dessert recipes.

Dessert is my favorite course, and as readers of my memoirs know, I have a formidable sweet tooth. My mother's maiden name is Baker, which is extremely *à propos* as I come from a long line of women who not only love baking but also love *eating* the delicious things we bake. I always get excited when we get to the dessert course, and I make sure to always leave a bit of room to enjoy it. I cannot fathom turning down a delicious dessert on the grounds of being full. Life is just too short to miss out on such pleasure.

In France, I discovered a whole new selection of indulgences, many of which you will find below. I adore how desserts in France are far less sweet and far more concentrated in flavor than their North American cousins. A little serving goes a long way and leaves all my taste buds and cravings satisfied.

# THE SWEET FINISH

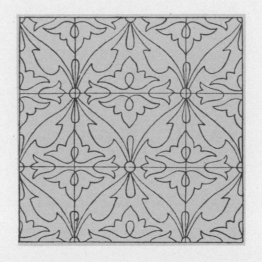

# MÉMÉ'S CHOCOLATE MOUSSE

## SERVES 4–6

This isn't strictly speaking Mémé's recipe. Let me explain. . .

Mémé must have shown me how to make chocolate mousse like she did over twenty times, but I screwed it up more often than I can count. Maybe I'm overly suspicious, but I am convinced to this day that she left out an ingredient or a step when she taught me. One time after Mémé tasted one of my botched attempts (I didn't know I had to wait for the chocolate to cool, so I essentially cooked the egg yolks), she patted my shoulder and said, "Don't worry, Laura, *ma belle*. You're very academic. Not everybody is cut out to be a cook." As far as I know, she only passed down her actual, complete recipes to Franck and his mom. . . and I'm not so sure about the recipes Franck's mom got. As for me, I received the incomplete, granddaughter-in-law version.

I finally searched around for other recipes, and I was given this one by my neighbor in Villers, Mme Fribourg. It looks tricky, but in fact all it takes is a bit of patience. It's also the closest to Mémé's mousse I have ever been able to make. I still feel this recipe has to be named after her, though, because she will be forever connected with chocolate mousse for me. She made the absolute best, and she would make it especially for me because she knew it was my favorite dessert. This, of course, is how I knew she loved me, despite her mischeviousness.

---

7 oz (about 1½ cups) good-quality semisweet baking chocolate

6 large eggs

¾ cup whipping cream

1 tsp pure vanilla extract

1 tsp icing sugar

---

Chop the chocolate into chunks and place them in a glass or metal bowl that fits into a medium-sized pot. Fill a medium pot halfway with water and place it over medium-high heat. Place the bowl with the chocolate on top. Bring the water to a gentle boil. Stir the chocolate until it just melts, remove the bowl from the pot, and stir the chocolate until smooth and shiny. Set aside to cool. (Alternatively, melt the chocolate for 1 minute in the microwave, then for an additional 15–20 seconds at a time until it is just barely melted. Stir until shiny and smooth.)

Separate the eggs. Place all the yolks in one medium-sized bowl and all the whites in another.

Add a pinch of fine sea salt to the egg whites, then, using a handheld or a stand mixer, beat them until they form stiff, shiny peaks, 3–5 minutes. Set aside.

Lightly whisk the egg yolks. Pour the cooled, melted chocolate slowly over them, whisking vigorously by hand the whole time.

Very gently, incorporate one third of the stiff egg whites into the chocolate and yolk mixture with a wide spatula, lifting and turning from bottom to top rather than beating it in. Incorporate the remaining egg whites.

Leave the mousse in the mixing bowl for a family-style dessert or spoon it into individual ramekins. Chill in the fridge, covered, for at least 1 hour before serving.

While the mousse is chilling, beat the cream and vanilla with the icing sugar until fluffy and stiff peaks form. Serve with the chocolate mousse.

# PEACH AND RASPBERRY CLAFOUTIS

## SERVES 6–8

Every French cook I know has a basic clafoutis recipe up their sleeve. Why? Clafoutis is basically a type of crêpe batter that's poured over a wide variety of fruits, so it's the perfect emergency dessert (which is great for me, as I tend to be rather. . . ahem. . . disorganized about meals). Luckily, it's so delicious that it makes the cook (i.e., me) look like they have been slaving over a hot stove for hours.

The most traditional clafoutis is made with cherries picked fresh off the tree. Franck's sister Stéphanie has a sour cherry tree and a black cherry tree in nearby Magny-les-Villers, so when we are in Burgundy during cherry season, we basically eat a clafoutis a day—and somehow never get tired of it. There is always a debate in Franck's family as to whether it is better to leave the cherries pitted or unpitted. I'll let you decide that thorny issue for yourself.

Last summer I received a bounty of peaches from a friend, so I decided to use those in my clafoutis. The result was so delicious, and the recipe so easy, that I had to include it here. Feel free to have fun with clafoutis and try any number of variations—plums, apples (maybe with some cinnamon?), berries of any kind. Your imagination is the only limit.

---

Heat the oven to 350°F. Grease an 8-cup (9-inch square) shallow baking dish with the butter and set aside. (Cast iron works great for this.)

In a large bowl, gently toss together the peaches, the 1 Tbsp of sugar, the lemon zest, and lemon juice. Add the raspberries and gently toss again to combine. Set aside.

In a medium bowl, whisk the eggs. Add the remaining ½ cup sugar, the flour, salt, milk, cream, and vanilla. Whisk well until all the ingredients are blended and the mixture is frothy.

Pour the fruit mixture into the prepared dish. Gently pour the custard mixture evenly over top.

Bake until firm, 45–50 minutes.

Let cool for 15 minutes. Dust with icing sugar and top with a dollop of whipped cream if you like.

1 Tbsp unsalted butter

4 medium-large fresh peaches, peeled and thinly sliced

½ cup + 1 Tbsp granulated sugar

2 tsp grated lemon zest

1 Tbsp lemon juice

1 cup fresh raspberries

4 large eggs

¾ cup all-purpose flour

¼ tsp sea salt

¾ cup whole milk

¾ cup whipping cream

1 tsp pure vanilla extract

Icing sugar for serving

Whipped cream for serving (optional)

---

*Clafoutis is best eaten the day it's made, but if you do have leftovers, pop the dish back in a warm oven for 15 minutes, then eat the clafouti like slices of pancake, drizzled with honey or syrup.—RW*

# RUSTIC CHERRY GALETTE

## SERVES 6–8

This recipe was inspired by my sister-in-law's beautiful cherry trees. When Stéphanie's trees are producing and we are not eating cherry clafoutis, we can be found eating cherry tarts. As with clafoutis, there is a huge debate about whether the cherries should be pitted. I witnessed a massive family argument about this between Franck's grandmother, Mémé, and his mother, Michèle.

Mémé was convinced that removing the pits detracted from the taste, whereas Michèle said leaving them just led to broken teeth and made no taste difference whatsoever. The battle resulted in Michèle storming away and a seriously uncomfortable atmosphere for this here conflict-averse Canadian. Luckily, I had my slice of cherry tart to distract me.

Rebecca cleverly upped the style and taste quotient of this tart by making it caramelized galette-style. Pits or not, this recipe will not disappoint.

2½ lb cherries

¼ cup granulated sugar

¼ cup cornstarch

2 tsp finely grated lemon zest

2 Tbsp lemon juice

1½ tsp pure vanilla extract

1 recipe Basic Pastry (sweet) (page 38)

2 Tbsp butter, cubed

1 egg, beaten

2 Tbsp brown sugar

Vanilla ice cream to serve

Line a large rimmed sheet pan with parchment paper.

Pit the cherries (or not—your preference).

In a large bowl, stir together the cherries, granulated sugar, cornstarch, lemon zest, lemon juice, and vanilla.

Roll out the pastry into a rustic circle, about ⅛-inch thick and 15 inches in diameter. Place it on the prepared sheet pan.

Pile the cherries into the center of the pastry, leaving a 2-inch border around the edges. Evenly scatter the butter cubes over the cherries. Fold the edges of the pastry over the cherries and toward the center, overlapping, in a pleated fashion, as you go around. Leave the cherries peeking through in the center. Brush the crust with the egg and sprinkle with the brown sugar. Refrigerate for ½ hour.

Heat the oven to 400°F.

Bake the galette until the crust is browned and the cherries are cooked and caramelized, 35–45 minutes.

Let rest for 15 minutes before cutting and then serve with vanilla ice cream.

# FRENCH APPLE CAKE

### SERVES 6–8

When fall rolls around and the air starts to become crisp in the mornings, my thoughts go to all things apple. This simple and delicious apple cake is perfect dipped in a cup of afternoon tea or coffee (and is also rather perfect for breakfast in the unlikely event you have any left over). The French love apple desserts, and as apples are fresh and inexpensive in so many parts of the world, this recipe adapts beautifully to almost anywhere.

---

Heat the oven to 375°F and generously grease a 9-inch springform pan. Place the pan on a parchment paper–lined rimmed sheet pan.

Peel and core the apples. Cut them into 1-inch pieces and toss well with the lemon juice so all the pieces are coated. Set aside.

In a small bowl, whisk together both flours, the baking powder, and salt. Set it aside.

In a large bowl, using a wire whisk, beat the eggs until well blended and foamy, and then whisk in the sugar, Calvados, and vanilla. Using a wooden spoon, stir in half of the flour mixture, then gently stir in half of the melted butter.

Gently fold in the remaining flour mixture, then the rest of the butter until the batter is well blended and there are no traces of dry flour. Fold in the apples until they're all well coated with the batter. Scrape the batter into the prepared pan and smooth the top a little with a spatula.

Bake until the cake is nicely browned and a toothpick inserted into the center comes out clean, 50–60 minutes.

Let the cake cool in the pan on a cooling rack for 10 minutes, then run a knife around the edge to loosen it from the pan. Carefully remove the sides of the cake pan. Let cool for another 15 minutes.

Sprinkle the cake with the icing sugar and then serve with ice cream or crème fraîche.

2 large apples, such as Honeycrisp, Golden Delicious, or Granny Smith

1 Tbsp lemon juice

1 cup all-purpose flour

2 Tbsp almond flour

1 tsp baking powder

¼ tsp sea salt

2 large eggs

½ cup granulated sugar

2 Tbsp Calvados liqueur

½ tsp pure vanilla extract

½ cup butter, melted and cooled to room temperature

1 Tbsp icing sugar

Ice cream or Crème Fraîche (page 30) to serve

# MARIE'S LEMON TART

## SERVES 6–8

This is one of those stalwart, life-saving recipes, like the chocolate cake on page 201. It isn't difficult, but it gets rave reviews every time. The first time I tried it was at my friend Marie's house in Beaune. She made it for dessert one dreary Wednesday when all of our kids were upstairs playing and just she, Franck, and I were having lunch together.

With the rain pattering on the windowpanes in a strangely comforting fashion, we drank many espressos after lunch, chatting and laughing—and before we knew it, the three of us had devoured the entire lemon tart. Its bright, creamy lemon zing is the perfect antidote to winter days. It is so much the quintessence of France you simply must surrender to the pleasure of eating it. The pastry crumbles apart quite easily, but just press and assemble it like puzzle pieces in the pan and it will be perfect.

Butter and flour for preparing pan

1 recipe Pâte Sablée (page 38)

¾ cup Crème Fraîche (page 30) or whipping cream

2 large eggs

½ cup granulated sugar

1 Tbsp all-purpose flour

1½ tsp finely minced lemon zest

3 Tbsp lemon juice

Heat the oven to 350°F. Butter and flour a 10-inch tart pan and set aside. Line a rimmed sheet pan with parchment paper.

Roll out the pastry to a circle about ⅛-inch thick and large enough to line the bottom and sides of your tart pan, and press it into the prepared pan. The pastry might be a bit crumbly but that's okay. Poke it all over with a fork so it doesn't puff up.

Cut a 10-inch circle of parchment paper and lay it in the center of the pan, over the dough. Cover the parchment with baking beads or dry beans. Place the pan on the prepared sheet pan and bake for 10 minutes.

Place a medium pot over medium heat and add the crème fraîche (or cream). Barely bring to a boil, whisking so it doesn't stick to the bottom of the pot. Watch carefully, as the cream will rise as it heats. Remove from the heat and set aside to cool to room temperature, 20 minutes, stirring occasionally.

In a medium-sized bowl, whisk the eggs with the cooled crème fraîche (or cream), the sugar, flour, lemon zest, and lemon juice. Pour this mixture into the pastry crust.

Bake until it doesn't jiggle in the middle, about 15 minutes.

Cool on a rack for 15 minutes, then move to the fridge and chill, uncovered, for about 20 minutes before serving.

*To make individual tarts as in the photo, prepare six 4-inch tart pans with removable bottoms. Use one pan to cut out six rounds of pastry, about 5 inches in diameter, and press each round of pastry into a tart pan. Because the individual tarts are small, there is no need to blind bake, but do prick holes in the pastry with a fork and bake for 10 minutes before adding the filling, then bake again for 10–12 minutes.*

# GERMAIN FRENCH CHOCOLATE CAKE

SERVES 8–10

In our household, this is *the* family cake. I make it for everyone's birthdays and for special celebrations, and my friends always ask me to make it for potluck dinners. Bonus: because it contains so little flour (only a tablespoon!) it is easy to make gluten-free by substituting gluten-free flour for regular flour.

Aude, a school friend in Burgundy, taught me how to make this decadent, rich-but-not-too-sweet concoction, and I've been making it ever since. I've taught each one of my girls how to make it and I've given countless friends and readers this recipe too. I've also given it a new name in honor of its status as a Germain family favorite.

I actually prefer it when it's had time to settle overnight in the fridge, so it's the perfect make-ahead dessert. It takes on a silky, dense texture that goes perfectly with whipped cream (I never sweeten mine), or a quick fruit coulis with minimal added sugar. It's great served slightly warm, and delicious and fudgy after a night or two in the fridge. After all these years of making this perfect cake, I'm confident it will become a tradition in your house too (with an optional name change, *bien sûr*).

Butter and flour for preparing the pan

7 oz good-quality semisweet baking chocolate, broken into chunks

¾ cup butter

1 cup granulated sugar

5 large eggs

1 Tbsp all-purpose flour

1 Tbsp icing sugar

Ice cream, whipped cream, or fresh fruit for serving (optional)

---

Heat the oven to 375°F. Butter and flour an 8-inch cake pan and set aside.

Place a glass or metal bowl over a medium-sized pot. Fill the pot halfway with water and place it over medium-high heat. Place the chocolate and butter in the bowl and bring the water to a gentle boil. Stir the chocolate just until it melts, remove the bowl from the pot, and stir the chocolate until smooth and shiny. Mix in the granulated sugar, and let cool for about 5 minutes.

Add the eggs to the chocolate mixture one by one, stirring well with a wooden spoon after each addition. Add the flour, and mix well to combine.

Scoop the batter into the cake pan and bake for 25–30 minutes. The cake should be slightly wobbly in the middle when taken out of the oven.

Let cool on a rack. Sprinkle with icing sugar and serve with ice cream or whipped cream and fruit (if using).

# PAIN D'ÉPICES

## MAKES ONE LOAF

Gingerbread is a traditional item in Burgundy, particularly in the town of Dijon. It's not the kind of gingerbread we associate here in North America with Christmas cookies, though. Instead, it's basically a spiced honey bread.

The prevailing belief is that it was imported from Flanders in the 16th century by Duke Philippe le Bon. Apparently he was so taken by the taste of it that he took the pastry cook who'd made it back with him to Burgundy (as a hostage or not, we'll never know).

As in medieval times, it is baked in either a loaf or in small rounds called *nonnettes*. My favorite way to eat it is dipped in coffee, but don't tell my mother, as she would be horrified by my bad manners. Whenever I eat gingerbread in Burgundy, I picture myself sitting at the high table at a medieval feast in a turreted castle, enjoying my gingerbread with mead in a bejeweled goblet. I advise you to do the same when you make this delicious recipe at home.

1 cup whole milk

½ cup honey

½ cup packed brown sugar

1 tsp ground cinnamon

1 tsp Quatre Épices (page 19)

1 tsp ground allspice

Zest of 1 lemon, 1 orange, and 2 limes in large strips

3 star anise

2 cups all-purpose flour

1 tsp baking powder

1 tsp baking soda

½ tsp fine kosher salt

1 large egg

¼ cup butter, melted and cooled

Put the milk, honey, sugar, cinnamon, quatre épices, allspice, zests, and star anise in a medium saucepan and bring to a simmer.

Remove from the heat, cover, and let steep for 25 minutes, stirring occasionally to help it cool. Strain through a fine-mesh sieve and discard the solids. Set the liquid aside.

Heat the oven to 400°F. Butter a 9- x 5-inch loaf pan.

In a large bowl, whisk together the flour, baking powder, baking soda, and salt.

In a separate large bowl, lightly whisk the egg. Add the milk mixture and melted butter to the egg and stir to combine. Fold in the flour mixture until just blended. Pour into the prepared loaf pan.

Bake until the loaf is deep brown and a toothpick inserted in the center comes out clean, 45–55 minutes.

Let the loaf cool in the pan for 15 minutes, then invert onto a cooling rack. Serve warm or at room temperature.

# FIG SORBET

## MAKES ABOUT 4 CUPS

Summers in Burgundy can be *hot*. We're talking 100°F and above. Sometimes it feels like walking straight into an oven on full blast. This is a far cry from the summers I experienced on my west coast island in Canada, where summer temps hover around 70°F and the cool wind off the ocean means we all head inside when the sun goes down. The summer heat in Burgundy always shocks me for the first few days and then I ease into a different type of eating and a different daily timetable. Often we don't sit down for dinner on our veranda until ten o'clock at night.

As a result, we like to eat things that cool us down in summer—such as this fig sorbet. The summer figs are glorious, and everyone seems to have a fig tree in their garden or to know of a secret one at the corner of a vineyard. You'll need an ice cream maker for this recipe.

2 lb ripe figs, halved lengthwise

2 Tbsp honey

¾ cup granulated sugar

2 Tbsp French brandy

1 Tbsp lemon juice

1 tsp sea salt

---

Heat the oven to 350°F. Line a rimmed sheet pan with parchment paper.

Set the figs, cut side up, on the parchment and drizzle with the honey. Roast for 20 minutes.

Meanwhile, combine the sugar and ¾ cup water in a small saucepan over high heat. Stirring constantly, bring to a boil, then remove from the heat.

When the figs are done, slide them off the parchment into a food processor fitted with the steel blade, scraping in any juices that may have accumulated on the paper. Blend until smooth, about 2 minutes. Pour into a large bowl. Add the sugar syrup, brandy, lemon juice, and salt and let cool completely.

Pour into an ice cream maker and, following the manufacturer's instructions, churn and blend until ready. This will keep in the freezer for up to 2 weeks.

# POIRE BELLE-HÉLÈNE

## SERVES 4

I tend to get frazzled when I'm cooking dinner for a group of people. My mind isn't linear or all that organized and executing a multi-course sit-down meal can quickly give me a case of overwhelm. I often say I would rather host a party for 100 people (good wine, good people, good music, and it's pretty much a guaranteed success) than a sit-down dinner for eight.

My solution is to stick to my tried-and-true favorites, which are all included in this book, and often when I'm short on time or energy I whip up a Poire Belle-Hélène for dessert. Poire Belle-Hélène is easy to execute and is met with unequivocal approval every time. Who doesn't like the flavor combination of pear, melted chocolate, and vanilla ice cream? Nobody, that's who.

½ cup granulated sugar

¼ cup packed brown sugar

1 tsp ground cinnamon

1 tsp vanilla

4 large pears with stems intact

½ cup semisweet chocolate chips

¼ cup whipping cream

Vanilla ice cream to serve

---

Place a large saucepan over medium heat and add ½ cup water. Add both sugars, the cinnamon, and vanilla. Bring to a boil, then turn down the heat to a simmer and let cook, whisking constantly, until the mixture is brown and slightly thickened, about 5 minutes.

Whisk in another 1 cup of water and bring to a simmer.

In the meantime, using a small paring knife, carve the core out of the bottom of the pears. Peel the pears, leaving the stems intact. Place the pears in the liquid and simmer, rotating occasionally, until the pears are tender when poked with a knife, 15–20 minutes. Remove from the heat and let the pears cool in the syrup.

In a small saucepan over low heat, use a rubber spatula to stir the chocolate chips with the cream until the chocolate melts and is nice and smooth, about 5 minutes.

Place a pear on each of four plates. Drizzle chocolate sauce over top and serve with ice cream.

# LEMON MOUSSE

**SERVES 8–10**

Delicious does not have to be complicated. I first tried this dessert when I was visiting family in Marseille, and I loved how the bright, vibrant taste of lemon made for a perfect dessert after a large lunch. We were sitting on the terrace of a restaurant overlooking the Mediterranean where fish boats bobbed about on the endless blue. I didn't think the day could possibly get better—sunshine warming my back, the salt of the ocean in the air, a salade niçoise in my tummy—but then the *garçon* brought me this lemon mousse and lo and behold, it did.

8 eggs, divided

¾ cup granulated sugar

1 Tbsp finely minced lemon zest

½ tsp kosher salt

½ cup lemon juice

1 cup whipping cream

Separate 4 of the eggs and set the whites aside.

Whisk together the 4 yolks, the 4 whole eggs, and sugar in medium-sized saucepan. Stir in the lemon zest, salt, and lemon juice until well mixed.

Place the saucepan over medium-low heat and cook, whisking constantly, until the mixture thickens, about 10 minutes. Transfer the mixture to a bowl, cover, and refrigerate until chilled.

In a medium bowl, beat the egg whites with a handheld mixer until stiff peaks form, 3–5 minutes. Fold these gently into the cool curd.

In a medium bowl, beat the cream until stiff peaks form, about 5 minutes. Fold it into the lemon mixture until fully combined. Spoon the mousse into serving cups or, if you plan to serve this family-style, a big bowl. Keep covered in the fridge until ready to serve.

# YOGURT CAKE

## SERVES 10–12

Yogurt cake recipes vary in France, but they are generally a French child's first foray into baking, although their introduction to the fabulous world of flavors begins much earlier. The French take the whole "educating the palate" thing extremely seriously (just check out the baby food aisles in French grocery stores to see what I mean).

My girls were no exception. This French yogurt cake was the first cake they ever made. The reason it is so easy for children (and adults. . . wink, wink) is that the yogurt cup is used as the measuring tool, so the kids don't have to distinguish ¼ cup from ⅓ cup, for example. We had to tweak the "yogurt cup" measurement system below, as outside of France a yogurt container can be a multitude of sizes. This gives you a recipe that can be used all over the world.

Many yogurt cakes don't use lemon zest, but I have always loved how it gives this cake a bright, fresh flavor. Rebecca has added a lemon glaze, which ups the tastiness and the beauty of this dessert. I would always let my kids decorate it the way they wanted. Some days they wanted to cut it in half and fill it with their French grandparents' pêche de vigne jam or confiture de lait (aka dulce de leche); other days they wanted to ice it and decorate it with Smarties. If you're short on time, it is also divine just plain or with a wee sprinkling of icing sugar.

---

Heat the oven to 350°F. Grease a 12-cup Bundt pan with butter or oil and sprinkle with flour.

To make the cake, in a medium-sized bowl, sift together the flour, baking powder, and salt and set aside.

In a separate small bowl, whisk together the yogurt, lemon zest, milk, lemon juice, and vanilla until smooth and incorporated. Set aside.

In a large bowl, using a handheld electric mixer (or use a stand mixer fitted with the paddle attachment), beat the butter with the sugar on medium-high speed until light and fluffy, 2–3 minutes. Add the eggs, one at a time, beating well after each addition. Scrape down the sides of the bowl.

Add one third of the dry ingredients to the butter mixture and mix on the lowest speed until just incorporated. Add half of the yogurt mixture and mix on low to combine. Add half of the remaining dry ingredients, mix to combine, followed by the remaining yogurt mixture, and then the remaining dry ingredients. Mix on low speed just to incorporate, scraping down the bowl as necessary. Do not overmix.

Pour the batter into the prepared baking pan and smooth the top with a spatula. Bake until the cake is golden brown and a toothpick inserted in the center comes out clean, 60–70 minutes. CONTINUED ON PAGE 213.

### Cake

Butter or vegetable oil and flour for greasing the pan

3 cups all-purpose flour

2½ tsp baking powder

¾ tsp kosher salt

¾ cup Greek yogurt

1 tsp grated lemon zest

⅓ cup whole milk

¼ cup lemon juice

1 tsp pure vanilla extract

1 cup unsalted butter, softened

2½ cups granulated sugar

3 large eggs

### Lemon Glaze

1 Tbsp unsalted butter

2 Tbsp lemon juice

1½ cups icing sugar

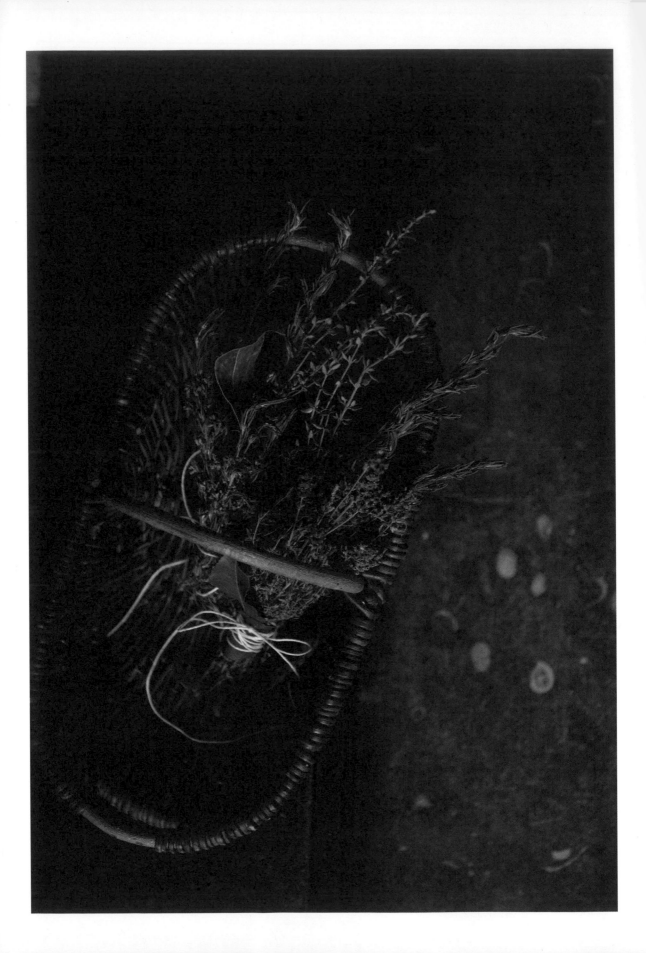

Remove from the oven and let cool in the pan for 15 minutes. Place a large cooling rack on top of the cake and carefully flip the entire thing, pan and rack, so the cake releases out of the pan and onto the rack. Let cool completely.

To make the glaze, place a small saucepan over medium heat and melt the butter. Whisk in the lemon juice, followed by the icing sugar.

Transfer the cake to a large plate and immediately drizzle with glaze. (Thin it with a teaspoon or two of warm water or wait a few minutes for it to harden slightly if it's not drizzling to your liking.)

This cake is typically best served the day it is baked, but it will keep in an airtight container on the counter for about 3 days.

# ACKNOWLEDGMENTS

First and foremost, I want to thank all the amazing cooks in France who have taught me recipes and regaled me with delicious food over the decades. You have shown me just how sublime the art of cooking can be. This means Mémé Germaine, of course, Michèle and André Germain, Stéphanie Germain, Renée Lobreau, Jean and Jacqueline Toutain, Charlotte Buffet (aka "Marie" in my Grape Series memoirs), Joelle Monette, Martial and Isabelle Henras, and my first host family in Burgundy, the Duperrets, especially Hervé who was a perfect guide for my introduction to the finer points of French *savoir-vivre*.

Thank you to the Rotary Club of Downtown Victoria for not sending me to Belgium on my exchange year, and for not dragging me back home to Canada when I moved in with my French boyfriend.

Thank you to the woman at Immigration Québéc in Paris who gave Franck his permanent residency papers to come to join me in Montréal on the basis that he was "madly in love." I wish I knew who you were so I could send you a photo of our three daughters.

Thank you to my parents, Lynda and Bryan, for putting up with me during my picky eater years, and for pretending not to notice when I fed my dinner to the dog under the table.

Thank you to Rebecca Wellman, my co-author, who has done such an amazing job creating, testing, and styling recipes and taking the wonderful photos that make this book so beautiful.

Huge *mercis* to Daisy Orser and Renate Wellman for being wonderful travel companions to France as well as impromptu models and cooking Sherpas. That day biking in the vineyards with you will forever be a favorite.

To our wonderful publisher, Taryn Boyd, for her faith in us and for just being a wonderful person to hang out with, as well as the entire team at TouchWood who invest their heart and soul in every book they publish.

More *mercis* to Lesley Cameron for her eagle editing eye, Tree Abraham for the stunning design, and Tori Elliott for her marketing prowess.

To Franck and our three daughters for being my loves and for maintaining a sense of humor about the fact that I was writing a cookbook. *Bah alors*, who's laughing now?

Lastly, to all my wonderful readers who have supported me through a transAtlantic move, a transplant, raising teenagers, eight books (so far), and who have been asking for this cookbook ever since *My Grape Escape* was published. I cannot tell you how delighted I am that *Bisous & Brioche* is finally in your hands. —LB

# INDEX

Edited by Lesley Cameron
Cover and interior design by Tree Abraham

CATALOGUING DATA AVAILABLE FROM LIBRARY AND ARCHIVES CANADA
9781771513166 (hardcover)
9781771513173 (electronic)

TouchWood Editions acknowledges that the land on which we live and work is within the traditional territories of the Lkwungen (Esquimalt and Songhees), Malahat, Pacheedaht, Scia'new, T'Sou-ke, and W̱SÁNEĆ (Pauquachin, Tsartlip, Tsawout, Tseycum) peoples.

We acknowledge the financial support of the Government of Canada through the Canada Book Fund, and the province of British Columbia through the Book Publishing Tax Credit.

This book was produced using FSC®-certified acid-free papers, processed chlorine free, and printed with soya-based inks.

Printed in Canada at Friesens

24 23 22 21 20    1 2 3 4 5